The Work
of Hans Loewald

COMMENTARY

"Hans Loewald is one of the handful of giants among analysts since Freud. Gerald Fogel has edited the first introduction and review of his work and it is outstanding. His introduction is sensitive and original. To several of Loewald's seminal papers, he has added helpful editorial notes. And he has included a fine general essay of his own to other valuable papers by Arnold Cooper, Lawrence Friedman, and Roy Schafer. All admire Loewald, but never uncritically; that is as it should be for any major figure. A fine book—needed by readers still unfamiliar with Loewald's thought; needed by analysts who have read his papers separately at separate times."
—**Vann Spruiell, M.D.**

"We all have the benefit of this masterful introduction to and overview of Loewald's work. It is admirably conceived and beautifully written, aptly enhanced by some of Loewald's most pivotal pieces. Not to know Loewald is not to know the richness of classical psychoanalytic thought in its most sophisticated modernity. Fogel's work on Loewald's thought is an estimable contribution."
—**Warren S. Poland, M.D.**

"Dr. Gerald Fogel's *The Work of Hans Loewald* is a remarkably innovative, thought-provoking, and informative book. The published work of Dr. Hans Loewald is evaluated as to its place in developing psychoanalytic theory, past, present, and future, including the once-elusive psychoanalytic theory of technique. His papers have been marvels of seminal value and clarity for several decades. Dr. Fogel has brought together a selected few, together with his own expositions—an appreciative, discriminating recognition of the centrality of Loewald's work to the future progress of psychoanalysis. Authoritative evaluations by Drs. Roy Schafer, Lawrence Friedman, and Arnold Cooper are here as well. This must become a source book and center for discussions by both students and seasoned practitioners."
—**Stanley L. Olinick, M.D.**

"Any practitioner whose clinical work is informed by the psychoanalytic model will find this an invaluable resource, placing the contemporary revolution in psychoanalytic technique in a historic and theoretical context and providing an introduction to one of its pioneers."
—**Robert Michels, M.D.**

The Work
of Hans Loewald:
An Introduction
and Commentary

edited by
GERALD I. FOGEL, M.D.

JASON ARONSON INC.
Northvale, New Jersey
London

Library of Congress Cataloging-in-Publication Data
The work of Hans Loewald : an introduction and commentary / [edited by] Gerald I. Fogel.
    p. cm.
  Includes bibliographical references and index.
  ISBN 0-87668-615-3
  1. Psychoanalysis. 2. Loewald, Hans W., 1906– . I. Fogel, Gerald, I.
RC506.W67 1991
616.89′17—dc20   90-22005

Manufactured in the United States of America. Jason Aronson Inc. offers books and cassettes. For information and catalog write to Jason Aronson Inc., 230 Livingston Street, Northvale, New Jersey 07647.

Contents

Chapter Five

Chapter Six

Chapter Seven

Chapter Eight

Chapter One

Loewald's Integrated and Integrative Approach

GERALD I. FOGEL, M.D.

Hans Loewald's greatest contribution may be as an integrator, although he is much more, as his many contributions are original and distinctive and go far beyond a synthesis of other people's ideas. What needs to be accounted for in Loewald, however, is how integrated and integrative the work is, how remarkably cohesive and unified, considering the diversity of his interests and complexity of his ideas. Integration, of course, is a central theme in his thought. In the last chapter I deal extensively with the apparent paradox that Loewald seems to embrace and to deepen long-standing traditions in Freudian psychoanalysis, somehow also to expand, challenge, and depart from these same traditions, yet never to lose the singular voice and unifying point of view that is his own. An important reason he can do this successfully is that he has two deep, but differing commitments. One is to what some call the "emerging paradigm" of the twentieth century, the worldview that has increasingly questioned the logically positivistic worldview of nineteenth-century natural science. The other is to the tradition of classical psychoanalytic methodology and practice. Intellectually and spiritually, Loewald is both a man of his times and an old-fashioned analyst, and he has reconciled the two without simplifying either.

Loewald's ability to reexamine both older and newer ideas deeply and respectfully, to find new ways to see them and their relationships to each other, and to shape them according to his unique sensibilities and distinctive personal voice all contribute to the integrative power in his work to which so many psychoanalysts have responded. He is one of the most seminal and influential thinkers in modern psychoanalysis, admired and quoted by analysts from a wide range of theoretical and clinical orientations. For example, both object-relational and classical ego-psychological theorists often claim him for their own. Sometimes an admirer focuses only on a portion of Loewald's ideas, however, mistakenly assuming that Loewald merely agrees with his own point of view. Loewald's actual reach is very wide, however. His work successfully integrates Freud and classic ego psychology with the developmental, self-psychological, object-relational, hermeneutic, and linguistic trends so influential in psychoanalysis today.

There is also a natural relation between his work and important contemporary ideas in the natural sciences, the humanities, and the arts. Some of these newer ways of thinking suggest, as Loewald's work does, a possibility of more effective interdisciplinary study than in the recent past— greater unification of knowledge and less reductionism when approaching one discipline from the point of view of another. Indeterminacy, relativity, chaos and systems theory, structuralism, phenomenology, existentialism—these nontraditional, nonlinear conceptual systems are sometimes intriguingly compatible with Loewald's approach to the traditional areas of study in psychoanalysis.

But one need not be familiar with any esoteric philosophy to understand Loewald, as he rarely strays from the conceptual premises and actual experiences of therapeutic practice. Along with his eloquent and evocative style, the grounding of his theoretical approach in the analytic situation is a major factor in accounting for his influence and appeal. Loewald's writings are demanding and complex, however, and sometimes difficult to penetrate, especially for those who do not have extensive experience and expertise in psychoanalytic theory and practice. Even many who appreciate his work probably do not fully understand it.

This volume should therefore fill a genuine gap, for until now there has been no careful review nor introduction to the work of this profound and highly regarded thinker. It is built around his important and most frequently quoted paper, "On the Therapeutic Action of Psychoanalysis" (1960). One can find almost everything in Loewald in this paper. In subsequent writings, he refines and elaborates on his basic theoretical ideas and principles, but this is the nuclear paper that crystallizes and unifies his thought, and predicts many of the ideas he will later pursue in more detail. Many regard this as one of the most challenging and important papers of modern psychoanalysis. The paper and its significance are reassessed in this volume by three major psychoanalytic thinkers: Arnold M. Cooper, Lawrence Friedman, and Roy Schafer. They consider its place in the history of psychoanalytic ideas, its relation to Loewald's other work, and the impact of Loewald's thinking on their own.

To introduce a reader to the wider scope of his work, Dr. Loewald requested that two other papers be included in this book. "Superego and Time" (1962) is a brief, accessible article that demonstrates how certain of his philosophic interests have influenced his views of psychic structure. "Psychoanalysis as an Art and the Fantasy Character of the Psychoanalytic Situation" (1975) is a self-contained contribution that reflects his conception of psychoanalytic treatment. I introduce each of these papers with a note explaining their significance in relation to Loewald's other writings, and I close the book with a detailed review and synthesis of the entire body of his work.

The more personal worldview that emerges from beneath the formal structure of Loewald's writings has profound implications for psychoanalysis. Loewald believes that a psychoanalysis that aspires to do justice to the human mind must respect empirical-deterministic methods and findings but must also reach beyond the limits of deductive logic to include additional dimensions. Psychic reality—human experience—is the proper domain of psychoanalysis, and psychic reality includes aesthetic, philosophic, and spiritual realms. Inspiration, passionate involvement, personal commitment, not always fully logical doubts, divergences, and allegiances— all of these regions are traditionally assigned to the heart or the soul, but they are actually provinces of the human mind. Psychoanalysis can legitimately attempt to understand and therefore speak out on such matters. In our clinical practices we attempt not to impose values and ideologies on our patients, but that does not mean we cannot admit and attempt to take into account the values and ideologies inherent in our views of the mind or implicit in our personal conduct of treatment.

Loewald often speaks frankly of such things, and his values and ideologies are implicit in most of his writings; in fact, they are among the significant sources of its strength. I think his work supports the idea that psychoanalysis, in its inability to be completely reduced either to science or humanity, may reveal not a limit but a strength. Psychoanalysis insists on the significance of process variables—existential and relational perspectives, as well as content variables more amenable to precise articulation and replication. Psychoanalysis may therefore have an important and meaningful role to play in the contemporary trend to seek a more integrated view of human nature and greater unification of human knowledge, for convergence and rapprochement between the natural and human sciences. Loewald's work is pathfinding in this respect.

Factors like these are reflected in Loewald's way of working, thinking, and writing. It is a way that has a long tradition in psychoanalysis. In recent years, such an approach has sometimes been subtly patronized by comparison to scientific method. The implication is that if we are ever finally to "verify" the findings and theories of psychoanalysis, it must be via outcome studies and other experimental research accessible to empirical verification. Empirical studies have value, of course, but can never substitute for the laboratory of personal experience that is the essence of and the "database" for much valuable psychoanalytic "research." Breakthroughs will always occur in this self-reflexive laboratory, as long as there are analysts willing to probe their hearts and minds in the privacy of their offices and at their writing desks.

There is a special, different kind of intelligence and discipline involved in this kind of research, which searches out truth in its own inevitable and necessarily creative ways. Work of this nature often is motivated by what Loewald describes in his Therapeutic Action paper as "the integrative experience longed for." When it is of high quality, such efforts will not only be scholarly, responsible, and responsive to reality, but also courageous, for courage is required when the truths sought cannot be obtained without personal risk and personal revelation, and where one must proceed without the absolute proofs that serve sometimes only as security blankets for scientific empiricists. When done well, such introspective research efforts often inspire, and also arouse deep feelings. Such phenomena cannot substitute for nor should they be idealized in comparison with scientific findings. But in the best instances, they augment and are inevitable accompaniments to the deepest intellectual convictions—those that reflect authentic and meaningful insights. Loewald's work always has seemed to me to represent this kind of psychoanalytic research at its best.

Perhaps this is why I have never hesitated to acknowledge the personal factor that was always so obvious when I considered the appeal of Loewald's writings to me. The person reflected in the writing—the ideals, values, and outlook on life of a psychoanalytic writer—are always factors in his persuasiveness and usefulness to others. Such factors add crucial perspectives to the manifest facts contained in a theory. I have no doubt that powerful subjective factors made me sense a deep affinity for Loewald's work, long before I could fully understand or explain why. We play unwitting roles in determining who we let teach us—on the basis of intuitive decisions made in advance of our conscious intentions or definitions of what is important and true. This is a reason why studying and presenting Loewald's work has been so deeply satisfying for me. For a psychoanalyst, theoretical growth signifies psychological as well as intellectual growth, and it cannot be done alone. Though I had never met him, Loewald was one of my important theoretical mentors, and therefore I inevitably see myself in relation to him in important ways when formulating my own theoretical points of view.

I recall the deep effect on me the first time I read the Therapeutic Action paper. I was in psychoanalytic training and was inspired, recognizing almost at once that I wanted to become this kind of analyst and thinker. I would read the paper many times, however, before I could explain it with any comprehensiveness or perspective. Though I understood little compared to what I understand today, that first reading was nevertheless a very valuable one. I later realized that Loewald is one of those writers who can be reread many times with pleasure and profit. Those who appreciate him will probably, as I have, find themselves returning to him again and again. I suggest to any who are coming to Loewald for the first time not to expect to absorb him all at once. After reading him you will return to other familiar works and professional activities and see old things in a new light; when you return again to Loewald, whatever new perspectives you have acquired will help you to see things there you never saw before. The chapters in the text that comment on Loewald can also be revisited with profit after deeper immersion in the original texts.

Loewald is developmental, existential-humanistic, and interpersonal, yet a classic ego psychologist with deep roots in Freud and the Freudian tradition. Object relations, preoedipal conflict, oedipal conflict, the mother–infant bond, narcissism, the self, trauma, empathy—all of these factors are taken into account. Loewald has quite naturally always brought these perspectives to bear on traditional psychoanalytic subjects, long before it was fashionable to do so. Almost always, the traditional concepts and newer ones are shown to have a wider context; in Loewald's hands each shapes, illuminates, and reveals new aspects of the other.

Regarding further reading: Though implicit in all his work, one thing that is not obvious in the chapter on therapeutic action is how central the concept of internalization will become in his system. Integral to the internalization concept is his conviction that there is an organizing tendency, a developmental thrust toward higher organization, a wish or a longing for psychological growth—for differentiation, integration, and unification. I would therefore suggest that to delve more deeply into Loewald after reading this introductory volume, one should next read "On Internalization" (1973).

The goal of gaining a comprehensive grasp of Loewald's theoretical system will also be served by reading the other two papers that figured prominently in the tracing of his theoretical evolution in my overview. They are "On Motivation and Instinct Theory" (1971a) and "The Waning of the Oedipus Complex" (1979). Also useful in this regard is his recent monograph, *Sublimation: Inquiries into Theoretical Psychoanalysis* (1988), where Loewald extends even further his thoughts on the nature of this underlying principle and natural tendency that ideally may transcend unity and differentiation in a higher organization. The important roles of symbolism, subjectivity, and illusion are also prominently discussed there.

I recommend additional further readings in the brief introductions to Loewald's other two papers that are included in this book. Most of Loewald's works that are discussed in the text are contained in his collected papers, *Papers on Psychoanalysis* (1980), which has recently been reissued in paperback.

Among the many pleasures in preparing this book was discovering that there are many other people in psychoanalysis who appreciate Loewald, and many of them appreciated my efforts to understand and characterize his work. Many sought me out. This led to new professional and personal friendships that might have seemed unlikely, because of the lines that often exist in our field on the basis of allegedly limiting ideological, political, and generational differences. As I have noted many times, Loewald's work builds integrative bridges that can make such barriers seem much less relevant.

Preparing this book has also brought me into contact with Loewald himself. Now in his eighties and no longer able to work at his prior pace, he remains intellectually vigorous, generous, humble, and quick to express gratitude for responsiveness to his ideas. It has been a great pleasure to know him in a more objectively personal way and an honor to have his collaboration in putting the book together.

Chapter Two

On the Therapeutic Action of Psychoanalysis

HANS W. LOEWALD, M.D.

Advances in our understanding of the therapeutic action of psychoanalysis should be based on deeper insight into the psychoanalytic process. By psychoanalytic process I mean the significant interactions between patient and analyst that ultimately lead to structural changes in the patient's personality. Today, after more than fifty years of psychoanalytic investigation and practice, we are in a position to appreciate, if not to understand better, the role that interaction with environment plays in the formation, development, and continued integrity of the psychic apparatus. Psychoanalytic ego psychology, based on a variety of investigations concerned with ego development, has given us some tools to deal with the central problem of the relationship between the development of psychic structures and interaction with other psychic structures, and of the connection between ego formation and object relations.

If "structural changes in the patient's personality" means anything, it must mean that we assume that ego development is resumed in the therapeutic process in psychoanalysis. And this resumption of ego development is contingent on the relationship with a new object, the analyst. The nature and the effects of this new relationship are under discussion. It should be fruitful to attempt to correlate our understanding of the significance of object relations for the formation and development of the psychic apparatus with the dynamics of the therapeutic process. A first approach to this task is made here.

Problems, however, of more or less established psychoanalytic theory and tradition concerning object relations, the phenomenon of transference, the relations between instinctual drives and ego, as well as concerning the function of the analyst in the analytic situation, have to be dealt with. I, at any rate, found it unavoidable, for clarification of my own thinking, to diverge repeatedly from the central theme so as to deal with such problems.

The chapter, therefore, is anything but a systematic presentation of the subject matter. The four parts of the chapter intend to light up the scenery from different angles, in the hope that the central characters will be recognizable although they may scarcely speak themselves. A more systematic approach to the subject would also have to deal extensively with the pertinent literature, a task I have found impossible to assume at this time.

Before I proceed, I wish to make it clear that this is not a chapter on psychoanalytic technique. It does not attempt to suggest modifications or variations in technique. Psychoanalytic technique has changed since the beginning of psychoanalysis and is going to continue to change. A better understanding of the therapeutic action of psychoanalysis may lead to changes in technique, but anything such clarification may entail as far as technique is concerned will have to be worked out carefully and is not the topic of this chapter.

I

While the fact of an object relationship between patient and analyst is taken for granted, classical formulations concerning therapeutic action and concerning the role of the analyst in the analytic relationship do not reflect our present understanding of the dynamic organization of the psychic apparatus. I speak here of psychic apparatus and not merely of ego. I believe that modern psychoanalytic ego psychology represents far more than an addition to the psychoanalytic theory of instinctual drives. In my opinion, it is the elaboration of a more comprehensive theory of the dynamic organization of the psychic apparatus, and psychoanalysis is in the process of integrating our knowledge of instinctual drives, gained during earlier stages of its history, into such a psychological theory. The impact psychoanalytic ego psychology has on the development of psychoanalysis indicates that ego psychology is not concerned with just another part of the psychic apparatus but is giving a new dimension to the conception of the psychic apparatus as a whole. I shall come back to this point later on.

In an analysis, I believe, we have opportunities to observe and investigate primitive as well as more advanced interaction processes, that is, interactions between patient and analyst which lead to or form steps in ego integration and disintegration. Such interactions, which I shall call integrative (and disintegrative) experiences, occur many times but do not often as such become the focus of our attention and observation, and go unnoticed. Apart from the difficulty for the analyst of self-observation while in interaction with his patient, there seems to be a specific reason, stemming from theoretical bias, why such interactions not only go unnoticed but frequently are denied. The theoretical bias is the view of the psychic apparatus as a closed system. Thus the analyst is seen, not as a coactor on the analytic stage on which the childhood development, culminating in the infantile neurosis, is restaged and reactivated in the development, crystallization, and resolution of the transference neurosis, but as a reflecting mirror, albeit of the unconscious, and characterized by scrupulous neutrality.

This neutrality of the analyst appears to be required (1) in the interest of scientific objectivity, in order to keep the field of observation from being contaminated by the analyst's own emotional intrusions; and (2) to guarantee a *tabula rasa* for the patient's transferences. While the latter reason is closely related to the general demand for scientific objectivity and avoidance of the interference of the personal equation, it has its specific relevance for the analytic procedure as such insofar as the analyst is supposed to function not only as an observer of certain processes, but as a mirror that actively reflects back to the patient the latter's conscious and particularly his unconscious processes through verbal communication. A specific aspect of this neutrality is that the analyst must avoid falling into the role of the environmental figure (or of his opposite), the relationship to whom the patient is transferring to the analyst. Instead of falling into the assigned role, he must be objective and neutral enough to reflect back to the patient what roles the latter has assigned to the analyst and to himself in the transference situation. But such objectivity and neutrality now need to be understood more clearly as to their meaning in a therapeutic setting.

Let us take a fresh look at the analytic situation. Ego development is a process of increasingly higher integration and differentiation of the psychic apparatus and does not stop at any given point except in neurosis and psychosis, even though it is true that there is normally a marked consolidation of ego organization around the period of the Oedipus complex. Another consolidation normally takes place toward the end of adolescence, and further, often less marked and less visible consolidations occur at various other life stages. These later consolidations—and this is important—follow periods of relative ego disorganization and reorganization, characterized by ego regression. Erikson has described certain types of such periods of ego regression with subsequent new consolidations as identity crises. An analysis can be characterized, from this standpoint, as a period or periods of induced ego disorganization and reorganization. The promotion of the transference neurosis is the induction of such ego disorganization and reorganization. Analysis is thus understood as an intervention designed to set ego development in motion, be it from a point of relative arrest, or to promote what we conceive of as a healthier direction and/or comprehensiveness of such development. This is achieved by the promotion and utilization of (controlled) regression. This regression is one important aspect under which the transference neurosis can be understood. The transference neurosis, in the sense of reactivation of the childhood neurosis, is set in motion not simply by the technical skill of the analyst but also by the fact that the analyst makes himself available for the development of a new "object-relationship" between the patient and the analyst. The patient tends to make this potentially new object-relationship into an old one. On the other hand, to the extent to which the patient develops a "positive transference" (not in the sense of transference as resistance, but in the sense in which "transference" carries the whole process of an analysis), he keeps this potentiality of a new object-relationship alive through all the various stages of resistance. The patient can dare to take the plunge into the regressive crisis of the transference neurosis that brings him face to face again with his childhood anxieties and conflicts, *if* he can hold on to the potentiality of a new object-relationship, represented by the analyst.

We know from analytic as well as from life experience that new spurts of self-development may be intimately connected with such "regressive" rediscoveries of oneself as may occur through the establishment of new object-relationships, and this means new discovery of "objects." I say new discovery of objects, and not discovery of new objects, because the essence of such new object-relationships is the opportunity they offer for rediscovery of the early paths of the development of object-relations, leading to a new way of relating to objects as well as of being and relating to oneself. This new discovery of oneself and of objects, this reorganization of ego and objects, is made possible by the encounter with a "new object" that has to possess certain qualifications in order to promote the process. Such a new object-relationship for which the analyst holds himself available to the patient and to which the patient has to hold throughout the analysis is one meaning of the term *positive transference*.

What is the neutrality of the analyst? I spoke of the encounter with a potentially new object, the analyst, which new object has to possess certain qualifications to be able to promote the process of ego reorganization implicit in the transference neurosis. One of these qualifications is objectivity. This objectivity cannot mean the avoidance of being available to the patient as an object. The objectivity of the analyst has reference to the patient's transference distortions. Increasingly, through the objective analysis of them, the analyst becomes not only potentially but also actually available as a new object, by eliminating step-by-step impediments, represented by these transferences, to a new object-relationship. There is a tendency to consider the analyst's availability as an object merely as a device on his part to attract transferences onto himself. His availability is seen in terms of his being a screen or mirror onto which the patient projects his transferences, and which reflects them back to him in the form of interpretations. In this view, at the ideal termination point of the analysis no further transference occurs, no projections are thrown on the mirror; the mirror, having nothing now to reflect, can be discarded.

This is only a half-truth. The analyst in actuality does not only reflect the transference distortions. In his interpretations he implies aspects of undistorted reality that the patient begins to grasp step by step as transferences are interpreted. This undistorted reality is mediated to the patient by the analyst, mostly by the process of chiseling away the transference distortions, or, as Freud has beautifully put it, using an expression of Leonardo da Vinci, *per via di levare* as in sculpturing, not *per via di porre* as in painting. In sculpturing, the figure to be created comes into being by taking away from the material; in painting, by adding something to the canvas. In analysis, we bring out the true form by taking away the neurotic distortions. However, as in sculpture, we must have, if only in rudiments, an image of that which needs to be brought into its own. The patient, by revealing himself to the analyst, provides rudiments of such an image through all the distortions—an image that the analyst has to focus in his mind, thus holding it in safe keeping for the patient, to whom it is mainly lost. It is this tenuous reciprocal tie that represents the germ of a new object-relationship.

The objectivity of the analyst in regard to the patient's transference distortions, his neutrality in this sense, should not be confused with the "neutral" attitude of the pure scientist toward his subject of study. Nevertheless, the relationship between a scientific observer and his subject of study has been taken as the model for the analytic relationship, with the following deviations: the subject, under the specific conditions of the analytic experiment, directs his activities toward the observer, and the observer communicates his findings directly to the subject with the goal of modifying the findings. These deviations from the model, however, change the whole structure of the relationship to the extent that the model is not representative and useful but, indeed, misleading. As the subject directs his activities toward the analyst, the latter is not integrated by the subject as an observer; as the observer communicates his findings to the patient, the latter is no longer integrated by the "observer" as a subject of study.

While the relationship between analyst and patient does not possess the structure, scientist-scientific subject, and is not characterized by neutrality in that sense on the part of the analyst, the analyst may become a scientific observer to the extent to which he is able to observe objectively the patient and himself in interaction. The interaction itself, however, cannot be adequately represented by the model of scientific neutrality. It is unscientific, based on faulty observation, to use this model. The confusion about the issue of countertransference has to do with this. It hardly needs to be pointed out that such a view in no way denies or minimizes the role scientific knowledge, understanding, and methodology play in the analytic process; nor does it have anything to do with advocating an emotionally charged attitude toward the patient or "role taking." What I am attempting to do is to disentangle the justified and necessary requirement of objectivity and neutrality from a model of neutrality that has its origin in propositions I believe to be untenable.

One of these is that therapeutic analysis is an objective scientific research method, of a special nature to be sure, but falling within the general category of science as an objective, detached study of natural phenomena, their genesis and interrelations. The ideal image of the analyst is that of a detached scientist. The research method and the investigative procedure *in themselves*, carried out by this scientist, are said to be therapeutic. It is not self-explanatory why a research project should have a therapeutic effect on the subject of study. The therapeutic effect appears to have something to do with the requirement, in analysis, that the subject, the patient himself, gradually become an associate, as it were, in the research work, that he himself become increasingly engaged in the "scientific project," which is, of course, directed at himself. We speak of the patient's observing ego on which we need to be able to rely to a certain extent, which we attempt to strengthen, and with which we ally ourselves. We encounter and make use of, in other words, what is known under a general title: identification. The patient and the analyst identify to an increasing degree, if the analysis proceeds, in their ego activity of scientifically guided self-scrutiny.

If the possibility and gradual development of such identification is, as is always claimed, a necessary requirement for a successful analysis, this introduces then and there a factor that has nothing to do with scientific detachment and the neutrality of a mirror.[1] This identification does have to do with the development of a new object-relationship of which I spoke earlier. In fact, it is the foundation for it.

The transference neurosis takes place in the influential presence of the analyst and, as the analysis progresses, more

---

[1] I am speaking here of "mirror" in the naive sense in which it has mostly been used to denote the "properties" of the analyst as a "scientific instrument." A psychodynamic understanding of the mirror as it functions in human life may well reestablish it as an appropriate description of at least certain aspects of the analyst's function.

and more "in the presence" and under the eyes of the patient's observing ego. The scrutiny, carried out by the analyst
and by the patient, is an organizing, "synthetic" ego activity.
The development of an ego function is dependent on interaction. Neither the self-scrutiny, nor the freer, healthier development of the psychic apparatus whose resumption is contingent upon such scrutiny, take place in the vacuum of scientific
laboratory conditions. They take place in the presence of a
favorable environment, by interaction with it. One could say
that in the analytic process this environmental element, as
happens in the original development, becomes increasingly
internalized as what we call the observing ego of the patient.

There is another aspect to this issue. Involved in the
insistence that the analytic activity is a strictly scientific one
(not merely using scientific knowledge and methods) is the
notion of the dignity of science. Scientific man is considered
by Freud as the most advanced form of human development.
The scientific stage of the development of man's conception
of the universe has its counterpart in the individual's state of
maturity, according to *Totem and Taboo*. Scientific self-understanding, to which the patient is helped, is in and by itself
therapeutic, following this view, since it implies the movement toward a stage of human evolution not previously
reached. The patient is led toward the maturity of scientific
man who understands himself and external reality not in
animistic or religious terms but in terms of objective science.
There is little doubt that what we call the scientific explora-
tion of the universe, including the self, may lead to greater
mastery over it (within certain limits of which we are becoming painfully aware). The activity of mastering it, however, is
not itself a scientific activity. If scientific objectivity is assumed to be the most mature stage of man's understanding of
the universe, indicating the highest degree of the individual's

state of maturity, we may have a vested interest in viewing psychoanalytic therapy as a purely scientific activity and its effects as due to such scientific objectivity. Beyond the issue of a vested interest, I believe it to be necessary and timely to question the assumption, handed to us from the nineteenth century, that the scientific approach to the world and the self represents a higher and more mature evolutionary stage of man than the religious way of life. But I cannot pursue this question here.

I have said that the analyst, through the objective interpretation of transference distortions, increasingly becomes available to the patient as a new object. And this not primarily in the sense of an object not previously met, but the newness consists in the patient's rediscovery of the early paths of the development of object-relations leading to a new way of relating to objects and of being oneself. Through all the transference distortions the patient reveals rudiments at least of the core of himself and "objects" that have been distorted. It is this core, rudimentary and vague as it may be, to which the analyst has reference when he interprets transferences and defenses, and not some abstract concept of reality or normality, if he is to reach the patient. If the analyst keeps his central focus on this emerging core he avoids molding the patient in the analyst's own image or imposing on the patient his own concept of what the patient should become. It requires an objectivity and neutrality the essence of which is love and respect for the individual and for individual development. This love and respect represent that counterpart in "reality," in interaction with which the organization and reorganization of ego and psychic apparatus take place.

The parent–child relationship can serve as a model here. The parent ideally is in an empathic relationship of understanding the child's particular stage in development, yet ahead in his vision of the child's future and mediating this vision to the child in his dealing with him. This vision, informed by the parent's own experience and knowledge of growth and future, is, ideally, a more articulate and more integrated version of the core of being that the child presents to the parent. This "more" that the parent sees and knows, he mediates to the child so that the child in identification with it can grow. The child, by internalizing aspects of the parent, also internalizes the parent's image of the child—an image that is mediated to the child in the thousand different ways of being handled, bodily and emotionally. Early identification as part of ego development, built up through introjection of maternal aspects, includes introjection of the mother's image of the child. Part of what is introjected is the image of the child as seen, felt, smelled, heard, touched by the mother. It would perhaps be more correct to add that what happens is not wholly a process of introjection, if introjection is used as a term for an intrapsychic activity. The bodily handling of and concern with the child, the manner in which the child is fed, touched, cleaned, the way it is looked at, talked to, called by name, recognized, and rerecognized—all these and many other ways of communicating with the child, and communicating to him his identity, sameness, unity, and individuality, shape and mold him so that he can begin to identify himself, to feel and recognize himself as one and as separate from others yet with others. The child begins to experience himself as a centered unit by being centered upon.

In analysis, if it is to be a process leading to structural changes, interactions of a comparable nature have to take place. At this point I only want to indicate, by sketching these interactions during early development, the positive nature of the neutrality required, which includes the capacity for mature object-relations as manifested in the parent by his or her ability to follow and at the same time be ahead of the child's development.

Mature object-relations are not characterized by a sameness of relatedness but by an optimal range of relatedness and by the ability to relate to different objects according to their particular levels of maturity. In analysis, a mature object-relationship is maintained with a given patient if the analyst relates to the patient in tune with the shifting levels of development manifested by the patient at different times, but always from the viewpoint of potential growth, that is, from the viewpoint of the future. It seems to be the fear of molding the patient in one's own image that has prevented analysts from coming to grips with the dimension of the future in analytic theory and practice, a strange omission considering the fact that growth and development are at the center of all psychoanalytic concern. A fresh and deeper approach to the superego problem cannot be taken without facing this issue.

The patient, in order to attain structural changes in his ego organization, needs the relatedness with a consistently mature object. This, of course, does not mean that during the course of the analysis the analyst is *experienced* by the patient always or most of the time as a mature object. In the analyst it requires the establishment and exercise of special skills during the analytic hour, similar in structure to other professional skills (including the fact that as a skill it is practiced only during the professional work period) and related to the special, but not professionally articulated and concentrated attitudes of parents when dealing with their children.

I am trying to indicate that the activity of the analyst, and specifically his interpretations as well as the ways in which they are integrated by the patient, need to be considered and understood in terms of the psychodynamics of the ego. Such psychodynamics cannot be worked out without proper attention to the functionings of integrative processes in the ego-reality field, beginning with such processes as introjection, identification, projection (of which we know something), and progressing to their genetic derivatives, modifications, and transformations in later life stages (of which we understand very little, except insofar as they are used for defensive purposes). The more intact the ego of the patient, the more of this integration taking place in the analytic process occurs without being noticed or at least without being considered and conceptualized as an essential element in the analytic process. "Classical" analysis with "classical" cases easily leaves unrecognized essential elements of the analytic process, not because they are not present but because they are as difficult to see in such cases as it was difficult to discover "classical" psychodynamics in normal people. Cases with obvious ego defects magnify what also occurs in the typical analysis of the neuroses, just as in neurotics we see magnified the psychodynamics of human beings in general. This is not to say that there is no difference between the analysis of the classical psychoneuroses and of cases with obvious ego defects. In the latter, especially in borderline cases and psychoses, processes such as I tried to sketch in the child–parent relationship take place in the therapeutic situation on levels relatively close and similar to those of the early child–parent relationship. The farther we move away from gross ego defect cases, the more do these integrative processes take place on higher levels of sublimation and by modes of communication that show much more complex stages of organization.

II

The elaboration of the structural point of view in psychoanalytic theory has brought about the danger of isolating the different structures of the psychic apparatus from one another. It may look nowadays as though the ego is a creature of and functioning in conjunction with external reality, whereas the area of the instinctual drives, of the id, is as such unrelated to the external world. To use Freud's archaeological simile, it is as though the functional relationship between the deeper strata of an excavation and *their* external environment were denied because these deeper strata are not in a functional relationship with the present-day environment; as though it were maintained that the architectural structures of deeper, earlier strata are due to purely "internal" processes, in contrast to the functional interrelatedness between present architectural structures (higher, later strata) and the external environment that we see and live in. The id—in the archaeological analogy being comparable to a deeper, earlier stratum—integrates with its correlative "early" external environment as much as the ego integrates with the ego's more "recent" external reality. The id deals with and is a creature of "adaptation" just as much as the ego—but on a very different level of organization.

Earlier I referred to the conception of the psychic apparatus as a closed system and said that this view has a bearing on the traditional notion of the analyst's neutrality and of his function as a mirror. It is in this context that I now enter into a discussion of the concept of instinctual drives, particularly as regards their relation to objects, as formulated in psychoanalytic theory. I shall preface this discussion with a quotation from Freud that is taken from the introduction to his discussion of instincts in his paper "Instincts and Their Vicissitudes." He says:

> The true beginning of scientific activity consists . . . in describing phenomena and then in proceeding to group, classify and correlate them. *Even at the stage of description it is not*

possible to avoid applying certain abstract ideas to the material in hand, ideas derived from somewhere or other but certainly not from the new observations alone. Such ideas—which will later become the basic concepts of the science—are still more indispensable as the material is further worked over. They must at first necessarily possess some degree of indefiniteness; there can be no question of any clear delimitation of their content. So long as they remain in this condition, we come to an understanding about their meaning by making repeated references to the material of observation *from which they appear to have been derived, but upon which, in fact, they have been imposed.* Thus, strictly speaking, they are in the nature of conventions— although everything depends on their not being arbitrarily chosen but determined by their having significant relations to the empirical material, relations that we seem to sense before we can clearly recognize and demonstrate them. It is only after more thorough investigation of the field of observation that we are able to formulate its basic scientific concepts with increased precision, and progressively so to modify them that they become serviceable and consistent over a wide area. Then, indeed, the time may have come to confine them in definitions. The advance of knowledge, however, does not tolerate any rigidity even in defintions. Physics furnishes an excellent illustration of the way in which even "basic concepts" that have been established in the form of definitions are constantly being altered in their content. [pp. 117–118]

The concept of instinct (*Trieb*), Freud goes on to say, is such a basic concept, "conventional but still somewhat obscure," and thus open to alterations in its content (my italics).

In this same paper, Freud defines instinct as a stimulus; a stimulus not arising in the outer world but "from within the organism." He adds that "a better term for an instinctual stimulus is a 'need,'" and says that such "stimuli are the signs of an internal world." Freud lays explicit stress on one fundamental implication of his whole consideration of instincts here, namely that it implies the concept of purpose in the form of what he calls a biological postulate. This postulate "runs as follows: the nervous system is an apparatus which has the function of getting rid of the stimuli that reach it, or of reducing them to the lowest possible level." An instinct is a stimulus from within reaching the nervous system. Since an instinct is a stimulus arising within the organism and acting "always as a constant force," it obliges "the nervous system to renounce its ideal intention of keeping off stimuli" and compels it "to undertake involved and interconnected activities by which the external world is so changed as to afford satisfaction to the internal source of stimulation" (pp. 118–120).

Instinct being an inner stimulus reaching the nervous apparatus, the object of an instinct is "the thing in regard to which or through which the instinct is able to achieve its aim," this aim being satisfaction. The object of an instinct is further described as "what is most variable about an instinct," "not originally connected with it," and as becoming "assigned to it only in consequence of being peculiarly fitted to make satisfaction possible" (p. 122). It is here that we see instinctual drives being conceived of as "intrapsychic," or originally not related to objects.

In his later writings Freud gradually moves away from this position. Instincts are no longer defined as (inner) stimuli with which the nervous apparatus deals in accordance with the scheme of the reflex arc, but instinct, in *Beyond the Pleasure Principle* (p. 36), is seen as "an urge inherent in organic life to restore an earlier state of things which the living entity has been obliged to abandon under the pressure of external disturbing forces." Here he defines instinct in terms equivalent to the terms he used earlier in describing the function of the nervous apparatus itself, the nervous apparatus, the "living entity," in its interchange with "external disturbing forces." Instinct is no longer an intrapsychic stimulus, but an expression of the function, the "urge" of the nervous apparatus to deal with environment. The intimate and fundamental relationship of instincts, especially insofar as libido (sexual instincts, Eros) is concerned, with objects, is more clearly brought out in "Inhibitions, Symptoms and Anxiety," until finally, in An Outline of Psycho-Analysis, "the aim of the first of these basic instincts [Eros] is to establish ever greater unities and to preserve them thus—in short, to bind together." It is noteworthy that here not only the relatedness to objects is implicit; the aim of the instinct Eros is no longer formulated in terms of a contentless satisfaction, or satisfaction in the sense of abolishing stimuli, but the aim is clearly seen in terms of integration. It is "to bind together." And while Freud feels that it is possible to apply his earlier formula, "to the effect that instincts tend towards a return to an earlier [inanimate] state," to the destructive or death instinct, "we cannot apply this formula" to Eros (the love instinct) (pp. 148–149).

The basic concept Instinct has thus indeed changed its content since Freud wrote "Instincts and Their Vicissitudes." In his later writings he does not take as his starting point and model the reflex arc scheme of a self-contained, closed system, but bases his considerations on a much broader, more modern biological framework. And it should be clear from the last quotation that it is by no means the ego alone to which he assigns the function of synthesis, of binding together. Eros, one of the two basic instincts, is itself an integrating force. This is in accordance with his concept of primary narcissism as first formulated in "On Narcissism, an

Introduction," and further elaborated in his later writings, notably in "Civilization and Its Discontents," where objects, reality, far from being originally not connected with libido, are seen as becoming gradually differentiated from a primary narcissistic identity of inner and outer world (see my paper "Ego and Reality," 1951).

In his conception of Eros, Freud moves away from an opposition between instinctual drives and ego, and toward a view according to which instinctual drives become molded, channeled, focused, tamed, transformed, and sublimated in and by the ego organization, an organization that is more complex and at the same time more sharply elaborated and articulated than the drive organization that we call the id. But the ego is an organization that continues, much more than it is in opposition to, the inherent tendencies of the drive organization. The concept Eros encompasses in one term one of the two basic tendencies or "purposes" of the psychic apparatus as manifested on both levels of organization.

In such a perspective, instinctual drives are as primarily related to "objects," to the external world, as the ego is. The organization of this outer world, of these objects, corresponds to the level of drive organization rather than of ego organization. In other words, instinctual drives organize environment and are organized by it no less than is true for the ego and its reality. It is the mutuality of organization, in the sense of organizing each other, that constitutes the inextricable interrelatedness of "inner and outer world." It would be justified to speak of primary and secondary processes not only in reference to the psychic apparatus but also in reference to the outer world insofar as its psychological structure is concerned. The qualitative difference between the two levels of organization might terminologically be indicated by speaking of environment as correlative to drives, and of reality as correlative

to ego. Instinctual drives can be seen as originally not connected with objects only in the sense that originally the world
is not organized by the primitive psychic apparatus in such a
way that objects are differentiated. Out of an "undifferentiated stage" emerge what have been termed part-objects or
object-nuclei. A more appropriate term for such prestages
of an object-world might be the noun "shapes"; in the sense
of configurations of an indeterminate degree and a fluidity of
organization, and without the connotation of object-frag-
ments.

The preceding excursion into some problems of instinct
theory is intended to show that the issue of object-relations in
psychoanalytic theory has suffered from a formulation of the
instinct concept according to which instincts, as inner stimuli,
are contrasted with outer stimuli, both, although in different
ways, affecting the psychic apparatus. Inner and outer stimuli,
terms for inner and outer world on a certain level of abstraction, are thus conceived as originally unrelated or even opposed to each other but running parallel, as it were, in their
relation to the nervous apparatus. And while, as we have seen,
Freud in his general trend of thought and in many formulations moved away from this framework, psychoanalytic theory has remained under its sway except in the realm of ego
psychology. It is unfortunate that the development of ego
psychology had to take place in relative isolation from instinct theory. It is true that our understanding of instinctual
drives has also progressed. But the extremely fruitful concept
of organization (the two aspects of which are integration and
differentiation) has been insufficiently, if at all, applied to the
understanding of instinctual drives, and instinct theory has
remained under the aegis of the antiquated stimulus–reflex
arc conceptual model—a mechanistic frame of reference far
removed from modern psychological as well as biological

thought. The scheme of the reflex arc, as Freud says in "Instincts and Their Vicissitudes" (p. 118), has been given to us
by physiology. But this was the mechanistic physiology of the
nineteenth century. Ego psychology began its development in
a quite different climate already, as is clear from Freud's
biological reflections in *Beyond the Pleasure Principle*. Thus it
has come about that the ego is seen as an organ of adaptation
to and integration and differentiation with and of the outer
world, whereas instinctual drives were left behind in the
realm of stimulus–reflex physiology. This, and specifically
the conception of instinct as an inner stimulus impinging on
the nervous apparatus, has affected the formulations concerning the role of objects in libidinal development and, by extension, has vitiated the understanding of the object-relationship
between patient and analyst in psychoanalytic treatment.[2]

III

Returning to the discussion of the analytic situation and the
therapeutic process in analysis, it will be useful to dwell
further on the dynamics of interaction in early stages of
development.

The mother recognizes and fulfills the need of the infant.
Both recognition and fulfillment of a need are at first beyond
the ability of the infant, not merely the fulfillment. The

------

[2]It is obvious that the conception of instinct as an internal stimulus is
connected with Freud's discovery of infantile sexuality as stimulating sexual
fantasies, which earlier he attributed purely to environmental seductive traumati-
zation. It should be clear, however, that the formulation of that problem in such
alternatives as "internal" fantasies versus "environmental" seduction is itself open
to the same questions and reconsiderations that we are discussing throughout this
chapter.

understanding recognition of the infant's need on the part of the mother represents a gathering together of as yet undifferentiated urges of the infant, urges that in the acts of recognition and fulfillment by the mother undergo a first organization into some directed drive. In a remarkable passage in the "Project for a Scientific Psychology," in a chapter that has been called "The Experience of Satisfaction," Freud discusses this constellation in its consequences for the further organization of the psychic apparatus and in its significance as the origin of communication. Gradually, both recognition and satisfaction of the need come within the grasp of the growing infant itself. The processes by which this occurs are generally subsumed under the headings identification and introjection. Access to them has to be made available by the environment, here the mother, who performs this function in the acts of recognition and fulfillment of the need. These acts are not merely necessary for the physical survival of the infant but necessary at the same time for its psychological development insofar as they organize, in successive steps, the infant's relatively uncoordinated urges. The whole complex dynamic constellation is one of mutual responsiveness where nothing is introjected by the infant that is not brought to it by the mother, although brought by her often unconsciously. And a prerequisite for introjection and identification is the gathering mediation of structure and direction by the mother in her caring activities. As the mediating environment conveys structure and direction to the unfolding psychophysical entity, the environment begins to gain structure and direction in the experience of that entity; the environment begins to take shape in the experience of the infant. It is now that identification and introjection as well as projection emerge as more defined processes of organization of the psychic apparatus and of environment.

We arrive at the following formulation: The organization of the psychic apparatus, on the basis of given neuroanatomical structures and neurophysiological potentiality-patterns, proceeds by way of mediation of higher organization on the part of the environment to the infantile organism. In one and the same act—I am tempted to say, in the same breath and the same sucking of milk—drive direction and organization of environment into shapes or configurations begin, and they are continued into ego organization and object organization by methods such as identification, introjection, projection. The higher organizational stage of the environment is indispensable for the development of the psychic apparatus and, in early stages, has to be brought to it actively. Without such a differential between organism and environment no development takes place.

The patient, who comes to the analyst for help through increased self-understanding, is led to this self-understanding by the understanding he finds in the analyst. The analyst operates on various levels of understanding. Whether he verbalizes his understanding to the patient on the level of clarifications of conscious material, whether he indicates or reiterates his intent of understanding, restates the procedure to be followed, or whether he interprets unconscious, verbal, or other material, and especially if he interprets transference and resistance—the analyst structures and articulates, or works toward structuring and articulating, the material and the productions offered by the patient. If an interpretation of unconscious meaning is timely, the words by which this meaning is expressed are recognizable to the patient as expressions of what he experiences. They organize for him what was previously less organized and thus give him the distance from himself that enables him to understand, to see, to put into words, and to "handle" what was previously not visible, understandable, speakable, tangible. A higher stage of organization, of both himself and his environment, is thus reached, by way of the organizing understanding that the analyst provides. The analyst functions as a representative of a higher stage of organization and mediates this to the patient, insofar as the analyst's understanding is attuned to what is, and the way in which it is, in need of organization.

I am speaking of what I have earlier called integrative experiences in analysis. These are experiences of interaction, comparable in their structure and significance to the early understanding between mother and child. The latter is a model, and as such always of limited value, but a model whose usefulness has recently been stressed by a number of analysts (see for instance René Spitz 1956) and which in its full implications and in its perspective is a radical departure from the classical "mirror model."

Interactions in analysis take place on much higher levels of organization. Communication is carried on predominantly by way of language, an instrument of and for secondary processes. The satisfaction involved in the analytic interaction is a sublimated one, in increasing degree as the analysis progresses. Satisfaction now has to be understood, not in terms of abolition or reduction of stimulation leading back to a previous state of equilibrium, but in terms of absorbing and integrating stimuli, leading to higher levels of equilibrium. This, it is true, is often achieved by temporary regression to an earlier level, but this regression is "in the service of the ego," that is, in the service of higher organization. Satisfaction, in this context, is a unifying experience because of the creation of an identity of experience in two systems, two psychic apparatuses of different levels of organization, thus containing the potential of growth. This identity is achieved by overcoming a differential. Properly speaking, there is no experience of satisfaction and no integrative experience where there is no differential to be overcome, where identity is simply given, that is existing rather than to be created by interaction. An approximate model of such existing identity is perhaps provided in the intrauterine situation, and decreasingly in the early months of life in the symbiotic relationship of mother and infant.

Analytic interpretations represent, on higher levels of interaction, the mutual recognition involved in the creation of identity of experience in two individuals of different levels of ego organization. Insight gained in such interaction is an integrative experience. The interpretation represents the recognition and understanding that makes available to the patient previously unconscious material. "Making it available to the patient" means lifting it to the level of the preconscious system, of secondary processes, by the operation of certain types of secondary processes on the part of the analyst. Material organized on or close to the level of drive organization, of the primary process, and isolated from the preconscious system is made available for organization on the level of the preconscious system by the analyst's interpretation, a secondary process operation that mediates to the patient secondary process organization. Whether this mediation is successful or not depends, among other things, on the organizing strength of the patient's ego attained through earlier steps in ego integration, in previous phases of the analysis, and ultimately in his earlier life. To the extent to which such strength is lacking, analysis—organizing interaction by way of language communication—becomes less feasible.

An interpretation can be said to comprise two elements, inseparable from each other. The interpretation takes with the patient the step toward true regression, as against the neurotic compromise formation, thus clarifying for the patient his true regression level, which has been covered and made unrecognizable by defensive operations and structures. Secondly, by this very step it mediates to the patient the higher integrative level to be reached. The interpretation thus creates the possibility for freer interplay between the unconscious and preconscious systems, whereby the preconscious regains its originality and intensity, lost to the unconscious in the repression, and the unconscious regains access to and capacity for progression in the direction of higher organization. Put in terms of Freud's metapsychological language, the barrier between Ucs and Pcs, consisting of the archaic cathexis (repetition compulsion) of the unconscious and the warding-off anticathexis of the preconscious, is temporarily overcome. This process may be seen as the internalized version of the overcoming of a differential in the interaction process described above as integrative experience. Internalization itself is dependent on interaction and is made possible again in the analytic process. The analytic process then consists in certain integrative experiences between patient and analyst as the foundation for the internalized version of such experiences: reorganization of ego, "structural change."

The analyst in his interpretations reorganizes, reintegrates unconscious material for himself as well as for the patient, since he has to be attuned to the patient's unconscious, using, as we say, his own unconscious as a tool, in order to arrive at the organizing interpretation. The analyst has to move freely between the unconscious and the organization of it in thought and language, for and with the patient. If this is not so—a good example is most instances of the use of technical language—language is used as a defense against leading the unconscious material into ego organization, and ego activity is used as a defense against integration. It is the weakness of the "strong" ego—strong in its defenses—that it guides the psychic apparatus into excluding the unconscious (for instance, by repression or isolation) rather than into lifting the unconscious to higher organization and, at the same time, holding it available for replenishing regression to it.

Language, when not defensively used, is employed by the patient for communication that attempts to reach the analyst on his presumed or actual level of maturity in order to achieve the integrative experience longed for. The analytic patient, while striving for improvement in terms of inner reorganization, is constantly tempted to seek improvement in terms of unsublimated satisfaction through interaction with the analyst on levels closer to the primary process, rather than in terms of internalization of integrative experience as it is achieved in the process that Freud has described as: Where there was id there shall be ego. The analyst, in his communication through language, mediates higher organization of material hitherto less highly organized, to the patient. This can occur only if two conditions are fulfilled: (1) The patient, through a sufficiently strong "positive transference" to the analyst, becomes again available for integrative work with himself and his world, as against defensive warding off of psychic and external reality manifested in the analytic situation in resistance. (2) The analyst must be in tune with the patient's productions, that is, he must be able to regress within himself to the level of organization on which the patient is stuck, and to help the patient, by the analysis of defense and resistance, to realize this regression. This realization is prevented by the compromise formations of the neurosis and is made possible by dissolving them into the components of a subjugated unconscious and a superimposed preconscious. By an interpretation, both the unconscious experience and a higher organizational level of that experience are made available to the patient: unconscious and preconscious are joined together in the act of interpretation. In a well-going analysis the patient increasingly becomes enabled to perform this joining himself.

Language, in its most specific function in analysis, as interpretation, is thus a creative act similar to that in poetry, where language is found for phenomena, contexts, connections, experiences not previously known and speakable. New phenomena and new experience are made available as a result of reorganization of material according to hitherto unknown principles, contexts, and connections.

Ordinarily we operate with material organized on high levels of sublimation as "given reality." In an analysis the analyst has to retrace the organizational steps that have led to such a reality level, so that the organizing process becomes available to the patient. This is regression in the service of the ego, in the service or reorganization—a regression against which there is resistance in the analyst as well as in the patient. As an often necessary defense against the relatively unorganized power of the unconscious, we tend to automatize higher organizational levels and resist regression out of fear lest we may not find the way back to higher organization. The fear of reliving the past is fear of toppling off a plateau we have reached, and fear of that more chaotic past itself, not only in the sense of past content but more essentially of past, less stable stages of organization of experience, whose genuine reintegration requires psychic "work." Related to it is the fear of the future, pregnant with new integrative tasks and the risk of losing what had been secured. In analysis such fear of the future may be manifested in the patient's defensive clinging to regressed but seemingly safe levels.

Once the patient is able to speak, nondefensively, from the true level of regression that he has been helped to reach by analysis of defenses, he himself, by putting his experience into words, begins to use language creatively, that is, begins to create insight. The patient, by speaking to the analyst, attempts to reach the analyst as a representative of higher stages of ego reality organization and thus may be said to create insight for himself in the process of language-communication with the analyst as such a representative. Such communication on the part of the patient is possible if the analyst, by way of *his* communications, is revealing himself to the patient as a more mature person, as a person who can feel with the patient what the patient experiences and how he experiences it, and who understands it as something more than it has been for the patient. It is this something more, not necessarily more in content but more in organization and significance, that external reality, here represented and mediated by the analyst, has to offer to the individual and for which the individual is striving. The analyst, in doing his part of the work, experiences the cathartic effect of "regression in the service of the ego" and performs a piece of self-analysis or reanalysis (cf. Lucia Tower 1956). Freud has remarked that his own self-analysis proceeded by way of analyzing patients, and that this was necessary in order to gain the psychic distance required for any such work (Freud 1954, p. 234).

The patient, being recognized by the analyst as something more than he is at present, can attempt to reach this something more by his communications to the analyst, which may establish a new identity with reality. To varying degrees patients are striving for this integrative experience, through and despite their resistances. To varying degrees patients have given up this striving above the level of omnipotent, magical identification, and to that extent are less available for the analytic process. The therapist, depending on the mobility and potential strength of integrative mechanisms in the patient, has to be more or less explicit and "primitive" in his ways of communicating to the patient his availability as a

mature object and his own integrative processes. We call
analysis that kind of organizing, restructuring interaction between patient and therapist that is predominantly performed
on the level of language communication. It is likely that the
development of language, as a means of meaningful and coherent communicating with "objects," is related to the child's
reaching, at least in a first approximation, the oedipal stage of
psychosexual development. The inner connections between
the development of language, the formation of ego and of
objects, and the oedipal phase of psychosexual development
are still to be explored. If such connections exist, as I believe
they do, then it is not mere arbitrariness to distinguish analysis proper from more primitive means of integrative interaction. To set up rigid boundary lines, however, is to ignore or
deny the complexities of the development and of the dynamics of the psychic apparatus.

IV

In the concluding part of this chapter I hope to shed further
light on the theory of the therapeutic action of psychoanalysis
by reexamining certain aspects of the concept and the phenomenon of transference. In contrast to trends in modern
psychoanalytic thought to narrow the term *transference*
down to a very specific limited meaning, an attempt will be
made here to regain the original richness of interrelated phenomena and mental mechanisms that the concept encompasses and to contribute to the clarification of such interrelations.

When Freud speaks of transference neuroses in contra-
distinction to narcissistic neuroses, two meanings of the term
transference are involved: (1) the transfer of libido, con-

tained in the ego, to objects, in the transference neuroses, while in the narcissistic neuroses the libido remains in or is taken back into the ego, not transferred to objects. Transference in this sense is virtually synonymous with object-cathexis. To quote from an important early paper on transference (Ferenczi 1909): "The first loving and hating is a transference of autoerotic pleasant and unpleasant feelings on to the objects that evoke these feelings. The first 'object-love' and the first 'object-hate' are, so to speak, the primordial transferences." (2) The second meaning of transference, when distinguishing transference neuroses from narcissistic neuroses, is that of transfer of relations with infantile objects on to later objects, and especially to the analyst in the analytic situation.

This second meaning of the term is today the one most frequently referred to, to the exclusion of other meanings. I quote from two recent representative papers on the subject of transference. Waelder, in his Geneva Congress paper "Introduction to the Discussion on Problems of Transference" (1956), says: "Transference may be said to be an attempt of the patient to revive and reenact, in the analytic situation and in relation to the analyst, situations and phantasies of his childhood." Hoffer, in his paper "Transference and Transference Neurosis" (1956) states:

The term "transference" refers to the generally agreed fact that people when entering into any form of object-relationship . . . *transfer* upon their objects those images which they encountered in the course of previous *infantile* experiences. . . . The term "transference," stressing an aspect of the influence our childhood has on our life as a whole, thus refers to those observations in which people in their contacts with objects, which may be real or imaginary, positive, negative, or ambivalent, "transfer" their *memories* of significant previous experiences and thus "*change the reality*" of their objects, invest them with qualities from the past.

The transference neuroses, thus, are characterized by the transfer of libido to external objects as against the attachment of the libido to the "ego" in the narcissistic affections; and, secondly, by the transfer of libidinal cathexes (and defenses against them), originally related to infantile objects, onto contemporary objects.

Transference neurosis as distinguished from narcissistic neurosis is a nosological term. At the same time, the term *transference neurosis* is used in a technical sense to designate the revival of the infantile neurosis in the analytic situation. In this sense of the term, the accent is on the second meaning of transference, since the revival of the infantile neurosis is due to the transfer of relations with infantile objects onto the contemporary object, the analyst. It is, however, only on the basis of transfer of libido to (external) objects in childhood that libidinal attachments to infantile objects can be transferred to contemporary objects. The first meaning of transference, therefore, is implicit in the technical concept of transference neurosis.

The narcissistic neuroses were thought to be inaccessible to psychoanalytic treatment because of the narcissistic libido cathexis. Psychoanalysis was considered to be feasible only where a "transference relationship" with the analyst could be established; in that group of disorders, in other words, where emotional development had taken place to the point that transfer of libido to external objects had occurred to a significant degree. If today we consider schizophrenics capable of transference, we hold (1) that they do relate in some way to "objects," that is, to prestages of objects that are less "objective" than oedipal objects (narcissistic and object libido, ego and objects are not yet clearly differentiated; this implies the concept of primary narcissism in its full sense). And we hold (2) that schizophrenics transfer this early type of relatedness onto contemporary "objects," which objects thus become less objective. If ego and objects are not clearly differentiated, if ego boundaries and object boundaries are not clearly established, the character of transference also is different, inasmuch as ego and objects are still largely merged; objects—"different objects"—are not yet clearly differentiated one from the other, and especially not early from contemporary ones. The transference is a much more primitive and "massive" one. Thus, in regard to child analysis, at any rate before the latency period, it has been questioned whether one can speak of transference in the sense in which adult neurotic patients manifest it. The conception of such a primitive form of transference is fundamentally different from the assumption of an unrelatedness of ego and objects as is implied in the idea of a withdrawal of libido from objects into the ego.

The modification of our view on the narcissistic affections in this respect, based on clinical experience with schizophrenics and on deepened understanding of early ego development, leads to a broadened conception of transference in the first-mentioned meaning of that term. To be more precise: Transference in the sense of transfer of libido to objects is clarified genetically; it develops out of a primary lack of differentiation of ego and objects and thus may regress, as in schizophrenia, to such a prestage. Transference does not disappear in the narcissistic affections, by "withdrawal of libido cathexes into the ego"; it undifferentiates in a regressive direction toward its origins in the ego object identity of primary narcissism.

An apparently quite unrelated meaning of transference is found in Chapter 7 of *The Interpretation of Dreams*, in the context of a discussion of the importance of day residues in dreams. Since I believe this last meaning of transference to be fundamental for a deeper understanding of the phenomenon of transference, I shall quote the relevant passages.

We learn from [the psychology of the neuroses] that an unconscious idea is as such quite incapable of entering the preconscious and that it can only exercise any effect there by establishing a connection with an idea which already belongs to the preconscious, by transferring its intensity on to it and by getting itself "covered" by it. Here we have the fact of "transference" which provides an explanation of so many striking phenomena in the mental life of neurotics. The preconscious idea, which thus acquires an undeserved degree of intensity, may either be left unaltered by the transference, or it may have a modification forced upon it, derived from the content of the idea which effects the transference. [pp. 562–563]

And later, again referring to day residues:

the fact that recent elements occur with such regularity points to the existence of a need for transference. It will be seen, then, that the day's residues . . . not only borrow something from the Ucs. when they succeed in taking a share in the formation of the dream—namely the instinctual force which is at the disposal of the repressed wish—but that they also offer the unconscious something indispensable—namely the necessary point of attachment for a transference. If we wished to penetrate more deeply at this point into the processes of the mind, we should have to throw more light upon the interplay of excitations between the preconscious and the unconscious—a subject towards which the study of the psychoneuroses draws us, but upon which, as it happens, dreams have no help to offer. [p. 564][3]

One parallel between this meaning of transference and the one mentioned under (2)—transfer of infantile object-cathexes to contemporary objects—emerges: The unconscious idea, transferring its intensity to a preconscious idea and getting itself "covered" by it, corresponds to the infantile object-cathexis, whereas the preconscious idea corresponds to the contemporary object-relationship to which the infantile object-cathexis is transferred.

Transference is described in detail by Freud in the chapter on psychotherapy in *Studies on Hysteria*. It is seen there as due to the mechanism of "false (wrong) connection." Freud discusses this mechanism in Chapter 2 of *Studies on Hysteria* where he refers to a "compulsion to associate" the unconscious complex with one that is conscious and reminds us that the mechanism of compulsive ideas in compulsion neurosis is of a similar nature (p. 69). In the paper "The Neuro-Psychoses of Defence" the "false connection" is called upon to clarify the mechanism of obsessions and phobias. The false connection, of course, is also involved in the explanation of "screen memories," where it is called displacement. The German term for screen memories, *Deck-Erinnerungen*, uses the same word *decken*, to cover, which is used in the above

---

[3]Charles Fisher (1956) recently has drawn particular attention to this meaning of the term *transference*. His studies of unconscious–preconscious relationships, while specifically concerned with dream formation, imagery, and perception, have relevance to the whole problem area of the formation of object-relations and the psychological constitution of reality.

quotation from *The Interpretation of Dreams*, where the unconscious idea gets itself covered by the preconscious idea.

While these mechanisms involved in the "interplay of excitations between the preconscious and the unconscious" have reference to the psychoneuroses and the dream and were discovered and described in those contexts, they are only the more or less pathological, magnified, or distorted versions of normal mechanisms. Similarly, the transfer of libido to objects and the transfer of infantile object-relations to contemporary ones are normal processes, seen in neurosis in pathological modifications and distortions.

The compulsion to associate the unconscious complex with one that is conscious is the same phenomenon as the need for transference in the quotation from Chapter 7 of *The Interpretation of Dreams*. It has to do with the indestructibility of all mental acts that are truly unconscious. This indestructibility of unconscious mental acts is compared by Freud to the ghosts in the underworld of the Odyssey—"ghosts which awoke to new life as soon as they tasted blood" (p. 553n.), the blood of conscious–preconscious life, the life of contemporary present-day objects. It is a short step from here to the view of transference as a manifestation of the repetition compulsion—a line of thought that we cannot pursue here.

The transference neurosis, in the technical sense of the establishment and resolution of it in the analytic process, is due to the blood of recognition, which the patient's unconscious is given to taste so that the old ghosts may reawaken to life. Those who know ghosts tell us that they long to be released from their ghost life and led to rest as ancestors. As ancestors they live forth in the present generation, while as ghosts they are compelled to haunt the present generation with their shadow life. Transference is pathological insofar as the unconscious is a crowd of ghosts, and this is the beginning

of the transference neurosis in analysis: Ghosts of the unconscious, imprisoned by defenses but haunting the patient in the
dark of his defenses and symptoms, are allowed to taste
blood, are let loose. In the daylight of analysis the ghosts of
the unconscious are laid and led to rest as ancestors whose
power is taken over and transformed into the newer intensity
of present life, of the secondary process and contemporary
objects.

In the development of the psychic apparatus the secondary process, preconscious organization, is the manifestation
and result of interaction between a more primitively organized psychic apparatus and the secondary process activity of
the environment; through such interaction the unconscious
gains higher organization. Such ego development, arrested or
distorted in neurosis, is resumed in analysis. The analyst helps
to revive the repressed unconscious of the patient by his
recognition of it; through interpretation of transference and
resistance, through the recovery of memories and through
reconstruction, the patient's unconscious activity is led into
preconscious organization. The analyst, in the analytic situation, offers himself to the patient as a contemporary object.
As such he revives the ghosts of the unconscious for the
patient by fostering the transference neurosis, which comes
about in the same way in which the dream comes about:
through the mutual attraction of unconscious and "recent,"
"day-residue" elements. Dream interpretation and interpretation of transference have this function in common: They both
attempt to reestablish the lost connections, the buried interplay, between the unconscious and the preconscious.

Transferences studied in neurosis and analyzed in therapeutic analysis are the diseased manifestations of the life of
that indestructible unconscious whose attachments to recent
elements, by way of transformation of primary into second-

ary processes, constitute growth. There is no greater misunderstanding of the full meaning of transference than the one most clearly expressed in a formulation by Silverberg, but shared, I believe, by many analysts. Silverberg in his paper "The Concept of Transference" (1948), writes: "The wide prevalence of the dynamism of transference among human beings is a mark of man's immaturity, and it may be expected in ages to come that, as man progressively matures . . . transference will gradually vanish from his psychic repertory." But far from being, as Silverberg puts it, "the enduring monument of man's profound rebellion against reality and his stubborn persistence in the ways of immaturity," transference is the "dynamism" by which the instinctual life of man, the id, becomes ego and by which reality becomes integrated and maturity is achieved. Without such transference—of the intensity of the unconscious, of the infantile ways of experiencing life that have no language and little organization, but the indestructibility and power of the origins of life—to the preconscious and to present-day life and contemporary objects—without such transference, or to the extent to which such transference miscarries, human life becomes sterile and an empty shell. On the other hand, the unconscious needs present-day external reality (objects) and present-day psychic reality (the preconscious) for its own continuity, lest it be condemned to live the shadow life of ghosts or to destroy life.

I have pointed out earlier that in the development of preconscious mental organization—and this is resumed in the analytic process—transformation of primary into secondary process activity is contingent upon a differential, a (libidinal) tension system between primary and secondary process organization, that is, between the infantile organism, its psychic apparatus, and the more structured environment: transference in the sense of an evolving relationship with "objects."

This interaction is the basis for what I have called "integrative experience." The relationship is a mutual one—as is the interplay of excitations between unconscious and preconscious—since the environment not only has to make itself available and move in a regressive direction toward the more primitively organized psychic apparatus; the environment also needs the latter as an external representative of its own unconscious levels of organization with which communication is to be maintained. The analytic process, in the development and resolution of the transference neurosis, is a repetition—with essential modifications because taking place on another level—of such a libidinal tension system between a more primitively and a more maturely organized psychic apparatus.

This differential, implicit in the integrative experience, we meet again, internalized, in the form of the tension system constituting the interplay of excitations between the preconscious and the unconscious. We postulate this internalization of an interaction process, not simply internalization of objects, as an essential element in ego development as well as in the resumption of it in analysis. The double aspect of transference, the fact that transference refers to the interaction between psychic apparatus and object-world as well as to the interplay between the unconscious and the preconscious within the psychic apparatus, thus becomes clarified. The opening of barriers between unconscious and preconscious, as it occurs in any creative process, is then to be understood as an internalized integrative experience—and is in fact experienced as such.

The intensity of unconscious processes and experiences is transferred to preconscious–conscious experiences. Our present, current experiences have intensity and depth to the extent to which they are in communication (interplay) with the unconscious, infantile experiences representing the indestructible matrix of all subsequent experiences. Freud, in

1897, was well aware of this. In a letter to Fliess he writes, after recounting experiences with his younger brother and his nephew between the ages of 1 and 2 years: "My nephew and younger brother determined, not only the neurotic side of all my friendships, but also their depth" (1954, p. 219).

The unconscious suffers under repression because its need for transference is inhibited. It finds an outlet in neurotic transferences, "repetitions" that fail to achieve higher integration (wrong connections). The preconscious suffers no less from repression since it has no access to the unconscious intensities, the unconscious prototypical experiences that give current experiences their full meaning and emotional depth. In promoting the transference neurosis we are promoting a regressive movement on the part of the preconscious (ego regression) that is designed to bring the preconscious out of its defensive isolation from the unconscious and to allow the unconscious to recathect, in interaction with the analyst, preconscious ideas and experiences in such a way that higher organization of mental life can come about. The mediator of this interplay of transference is the analyst who, as a contemporary object, offers himself to the patient's unconscious as a necessary point of attachment for a transference. As a contemporary object, the analyst represents a psychic apparatus whose secondary process organization is stable and capable of controlled regression so that he is optimally in communication with both his own and the patient's unconscious, so as to serve as a reliable mediator and partner of communication, of transference between unconscious and preconscious, and thus of higher, interpenetrating organization of both.

The integration of ego and reality consists in, and the continued integrity of ego and reality depends on, transference of unconscious processes and "contents" onto new experiences and objects of contemporary life. In pathological transferences the transformation of primary into secondary processes and the continued interplay between them has been replaced by superimpositions of secondary on primary processes, so that they exist side by side, isolated from each other. Freud has described this constellation in his paper "The Unconscious" (pp. 175–176): "Actually there is no lifting of the repression until the conscious idea, after the resistances have been overcome, has *entered into connection* with the unconscious memory trace. It is only through the making conscious of the latter itself that success is achieved" (italics mine). In an analytic interpretation "the identity of the information given to the patient with his repressed memory is only apparent. To have heard something and to have experienced something are in their psychological nature two different things, even though the content of both is the same." And later (p. 201) in the same paper, Freud speaks of the thing-cathexes of objects in the Ucs, whereas the "conscious presentation comprises the presentation of the thing [thing cathexis] plus the presentation of the word belonging to it." And further: "The system Pcs comes about by this thing-presentation being hypercathected through being linked with the word-presentations corresponding to it. It is these hypercathexes, we may suppose, that bring about a higher psychical organization and make it possible for the primary process to be succeeded by the secondary process which is dominant in the Pcs. Now, too, we are in a position to state precisely what it is that repression denies to the rejected presentation in the transference neuroses: What it denies to the presentation is translation into words which shall remain attached to the object" (p. 202).

The correspondence of verbal ideas to concrete ideas, that is, to thing-cathexes in the unconscious, is mediated to the developing infantile psychic apparatus by the adult environment. The hypercathexes that "bring about a higher psychical organization," consisting in a linking up of unconscious memory traces with verbal ideas corresponding to them, are, in early ego development, due to the organizing interaction between primary process activity of the infantile psychic apparatus and secondary process activity of the child's environment. The terms *differential* and *libidinal tension system*, which I used earlier, designate energy aspects of this interaction, sources of energy of such hypercathexes. Freud clearly approached the problem of interaction between psychic apparatuses of different levels of organization when he spoke of the linking up of concrete ideas in the unconscious with verbal ideas as constituting the hypercathexes that "bring about a higher psychical organization." For this "linking up" is the same phenomenon as the mediation of higher organization, of preconscious mental activity, on the part of the child's environment, to the infantile psychic apparatus (cf. Charles Rycroft 1956). Verbal ideas are representatives of preconscious activity, representatives of special importance because of the special role language plays in the higher development of the psychic apparatus, but they are, of course, not the only ones. Such linking up occurring in the interaction process becomes increasingly internalized as the interplay and communication between unconscious and preconscious within the psychic apparatus. The need for resumption of such mediating interaction in analysis, so that new internalizations may become possible and internal interaction be reactivated, results from the pathological degree of isolation between unconscious and preconscious, or—to speak in terms of a later terminology—from the development of defense processes of such proportions that the ego, rather than maintaining or extending its organization of the realm of the id, excludes more and more from its reach.

It should be apparent that a view of transference, which stresses the need of the unconscious for transference, for a point of attachment for a transference in the preconscious, by which primary process is transformed into secondary process—implies the notion that psychic health has to do with an optimal, although by no means necessarily conscious, communication between unconscious and preconscious, between the infantile, archaic stages and structures of the psychic apparatus and its later stages and structures of organization. And further, that the unconscious is capable of change and, as Freud says, "accessible to the impressions of life" ("The Unconscious," p. 190) and of the preconscious. Where repression is lifted and unconscious and preconscious are again in communication, infantile object and contemporary object may be united into one—a truly new object as both unconscious and preconscious are changed by their mutual communication. The object that helps to bring this about in therapy, the analyst, mediates this union—a new version of the way in which transformation of primary into secondary processes opened up in childhood, through mediation of higher organization by way of early object-relations.

A few words about transference and the so-called real relationship between patient and analyst. It has been said repeatedly that one should distinguish transference (and countertransference) between patient and analyst in the analytic situation from the realistic relationship between the two. I fully agree. However, it is implied in such statements that the realistic relationship between patient and analyst has nothing to do with transference. I hope to have made the point in the present discussion that there is neither such a thing as reality nor a real relationship, without transference. Any "real relationship" involves transfer of unconscious images to present-day objects. In fact, present-day objects are objects, and thus real, in the full sense of the word (which comprises the unity of unconscious memory traces and preconscious idea) only to the extent to which this transference, in the sense of transformational interplay between unconscious and preconscious, is realized. The resolution of the transference at the termination of an analysis means resolution of the transference neurosis, and thereby of the transference distortions. This includes the recognition of the limited nature of any human relationship and of the specific limitations of the patient–analyst relationship. But the new object-relationship with the analyst, which is gradually being built in the course of the analysis and constitutes the real relationship between patient and analyst, and which serves as a focal point for the establishment of healthier object-relations in the patient's "real" life, is not devoid of transference in the sense clarified in this paper. I said earlier: To the extent to which the patient develops a "positive transference" (not in the sense of transference as resistance, but in the sense of that "transference," which carries the whole process of an analysis) he keeps this potentiality of a new object-relationship alive through all the various stages of resistance. This meaning of positive transference tends to be discredited in modern analytic writing and teaching, although not in treatment itself.

Freud, like any man who does not sacrifice the complexity of life to the deceptive simplicity of rigid concepts, has said a good many contradictory things. He can be quoted in support of many different ideas. May I, at the end, quote him in support of mine?

He writes to Jung on December 6, 1906 (Sigmund Freud and C. G. Jung, *Briefwechsel: The Freud/Jung Letters*):

I have kept to myself some things that might be said about the therapy's limits and mechanisms, or have presented them in a way that only the initiate recognizes. It will not have escaped *you* that our cures come about by the fixation of libido ruling in the unconscious (transference), which, to be sure, meets us more reliably in hysteria. It is this that provides the driving force [*Triebkraft*] for the understanding and translation of the unconscious; where this is withheld, the patient does not take the trouble or does not listen to us when we present to him the translation we have found. It is actually a cure through love. Transference then, too, provides the strongest, the one unassailable proof that neurosis is determined by man's love life [my translation from the original German text]. [p. 13; pp. 12–13]

And he writes to Ferenczi on January 10, 1910 (Jones 1955):

I will present you with some theory that has occurred to me while reading your analysis [referring to Ferenczi's self-analysis of a dream]. It seems to me that in our influencing of the sexual impulses we cannot achieve anything other than exchanges and displacements, never renunciation, relinquishment or the resolution of a complex (Strictly secret!). When someone brings out his infantile complexes he has saved a part of them (the affect) in a current form (transference). He has shed a skin and leaves it for the analyst. God forbid that he should now be naked, without a skin! [p. 496]

Chapter Three

Our Changing Views of the Therapeutic Action of Psychoanalysis

ARNOLD M. COOPER, M.D.

Hans Loewald is one of those rare figures in psychoanalysis who have managed to be intellectual revolutionaries with none of the trappings that usually accompany a revolution. His significant conflicts with and contradictions of more traditional ideas are put forward with no indication of combative spirit, although his presentation is forceful and his conviction is profound. It is likely that this conservative style of revolution has disguised the full depth of his disagreements with traditional analysis, and this may have delayed our benefiting from his ideas. Loewald's psychoanalytic position and his critique of classical psychoanalysis seem to be close in significant respects to views put forth by Sullivan, Klein, Rado, and more recently by Kohut; yet he never attracted to himself the rather harsh storms that broke over each of them in America. In 1959 Kardiner, Karush, and Ovesey's polemically phrased critique of libido theory was unacceptable to the usual analytic journals. Only a year later, however, Loewald's "On the therapeutic action of psychoanalysis," which was at least as encompassing although more subtle in its rejection of standard metapsychology, was published in *The International Journal of Psycho-Analysis*.

Loewald's vigorous conservative style also led him to a

defense of the traditional language of psychoanalysis. He said (1978a), "What psychoanalysis needs might not be a 'new language' but a less inhibited, less pedantic and narrow understanding and interpretation of its current language, leading to elaborations and transformations of the meanings of concepts, theoretical formulations, or definitions that may or may not have been envisaged by Freud. Words, including concepts used in science, are living and enlivening entities in their authentic function" (p. 193).

The expansion and redefinition of old terms is characteristic of Loewald's work. While this retention of our traditional language may have helped shield him from major controversy, it may also have obscured the freshness of much that he was telling us and blunted the full implication of some of his thought. Furthermore, I believe that we have now reached the point that increasingly imaginative use of existing language has so overburdened our lexicon that we no longer know which version of a concept is being used by each individual in a discourse (Cooper 1986). While this is desirable in poetry, at some point it becomes a problem in science and even in philosophy. As I will indicate later, however, Loewald may be more committed to the poetic rather than to the scientific vision of psychoanalysis. I will suggest that he uses two different languages that, although complementary, are not integrated and may not permit integration.

The title of Loewald's paper, written in 1957 and published in 1960, "On the Therapeutic Action of Psychoanalysis," invites comparison with Strachey's 1934 paper "The Nature of the Therapeutic Action of Psycho-analysis." I assume that Loewald had that in mind when he wrote his paper. Each of these papers represents an attempt to use the most modern concepts then available in psychoanalysis as a basis for reexamining its clinical core. A review of these two landmark papers may serve as a useful gauge of the profound changes that have taken place in psychoanalytic theory during the past half century.

Strachey, writing while Freud was alive and active, makes clear that he is writing out of the established psychoanalytic tradition of resistance analysis as explicated by Freud in the technical papers of 1911 to 1915. He is able to take for granted that the power of the analytic situation derives from the power of transference and that the efficacy of analysis depends upon the use of interpretation. He notes that little has been written by Freud on the topic of analytic technique since the *Introductory Lectures* when, as Strachey (1934) summarizes Freud, "he held that the ultimate factor in the therapeutic action of psycho-analysis was suggestion on the part of the analyst acting upon the patient's ego in such a way as to make it more tolerant of the libidinal trends" (p. 133). The new discovery that has prompted Strachey's attempt to reformulate the action of psychoanalysis has been the elucidation of the superego by Freud as part of the general advance of ego psychology. Strachey's aim is to reexamine the therapeutic process in the light of this new knowledge of the superego, and he attributes to Rado the idea of emphasizing "the notion of the super-ego as the fulcrum of psychotherapy" (p. 135).

Using a Kleinian perspective, Strachey (1934) believes that neurosis is a vicious cycle of the creation of hostile introjects secondary to the child's own hostile oral aggression, creating a harsh superego, with subsequent projection of aspects of these orally aggressive introjected objects back onto the external object, which will now be experienced as dangerous and frightening. This will, in self-defense, elicit even more destructive impulses toward the object, leading to an even more destructive introject. The way out of this vicious circle is through the modification of the superego:

If, for instance, the patient could be made less frightened of his super-ego or introjected object, he would project less terrifying imagos on to the outer object and would therefore have less need to feel hostility towards it; the object which he then introjected would in turn be less savage in its pressure upon the id-impulses, which would be able to lose something of their primitive ferocity. In short, a *benign* circle would be set up instead of the vicious one [and] his super-ego will be comparatively mild and his ego will have a relatively undistorted contact with reality. [p. 138]

The goal is marvelously clear. How is it achieved? Relatively simply. There are three steps:

1. The patient in analysis transfers the bulk of his id impulses onto the analyst.

2. "Owing to the peculiarities of the analytic circumstances and of the analyst's behavior, the introjected imago of the analyst tends in part to be rather definitely separated off from the rest of the patient's super-ego" (p. 140). As a result, following Rado's suggestion, the analyst becomes an "auxiliary super-ego" whose "advice to the ego is consistently based upon *real* and *contemporary* considerations and this in itself serves to differentiate it from the greater part of the original super-ego" (p. 140).

3. Under these circumstances the analyst is able to give mutative interpretations that break the vicious circle of hostile introjects and hostile projections. Mutative interpretations are given in two stages: (a) the patient's id impulses toward the analyst are interpreted and made conscious; and (b) the patient becomes aware that his primary hostile id impulses are directed toward archaic fantasy objects and not at real objects as represented by the analyst.

Only transference interpretations are mutative. Mutative interpretations must be exact; they work in small increments and represent small doses of reality that in time change the superego, breaking the vicious circle.

This model of therapeutic action seems straightforward, based on classical instinct theory and resistance analysis, and interlarded with a bit of Kleinian object relations theory. The role of the analyst is as a neutral, benign interpreter of reality, internalized as a temporary new object, helping to make the unconscious conscious, and modifying the superego. Classical analytic neutrality is preserved.

Loewald begins where Strachey leaves off. Because Loewald is such a vivid literary stylist when he speaks of therapy, I will quote him extensively, not only from the paper on therapeutic action but also from several other of his relevant papers that amplify the issues that concern us. Where Strachey drew on emerging knowledge of the superego as the basis for a new explanation of therapy, Loewald uses new ideas of interpersonal interaction and communication as his inspiration for a new description of the method of analytic therapy. He says (1960):

> Today, after more than fifty years of psychoanalytic investigation and practice, we are in a position to appreciate, if not to understand better, the role that interaction with environment plays in the formation, development, and continued integrity of the psychic apparatus. [p. 221]
>
> In an analysis, I believe, we have opportunities to observe and investigate primitive as well as more advanced interaction processes, that is, interactions between patient and analyst which lead to or form steps in ego integration and disintegration. Such interactions, which I shall call integrative

(and disintegrative) experiences, occur many times but do not often as such become the focus of our attention and observation, and go unnoticed. Apart from the difficulty for the analyst of self-observation while in interaction with his patient, there seems to be a specific reason, stemming from theoretical bias, why such interactions not only go unnoticed but frequently are denied. The theoretical bias is the view of the psychic apparatus as a closed system. Thus the analyst is seen, not as a coactor on the analytic stage on which the childhood development, culminating in the infantile neurosis, is restaged and reactivated in the development, crystallization and resolution of the transference neurosis, but as a reflecting mirror, albeit of the unconscious, and characterized by scrupulous neutrality. [p. 223]

The analytic stance that Strachey assumed as the norm—the benignly neutral analyst interpreting reality to counteract and correct the harsh superego—is greatly expanded into an explicitly interactive role, which is a rejection of the traditional "mirror" metaphor for the analyst.

To understand better what Loewald means by the role of interaction both in development and in analysis, it is necessary to examine some of his other writings on the topic. Throughout his work Loewald is explicit in claiming that all of psychic life consists of actual and internalized interactions. He goes to the heart of the psychoanalytic matter, and he drastically reformulates the instinctual basis of motivation as an interactive process. He (1971a) defines instincts as "forces within the psychic organization and not stimuli which operate on that system from without" (p. 123). "Instinct in psychoanalysis must be understood as a psychological concept" (p. 126). "The following thesis is proposed: instincts understood as psychic motivational forces become organized as such through interactions within a psychic field consisting originally of the mother-child (psychic) unit. (This formulation implies that neither objects nor instincts are any longer taken as givens or as concepts simply appropriated from other sciences.)" (pp. 127–128). "Thus I conceive instincts (considered in the framework of psychoanalytic psychology) and the id as a psychic structure, as originating in interactions of the infantile organism and its human environment (mother)" (1978c, p. 208). Although Loewald tries to justify this new usage of the term *instinct* through a sophisticated reading of Freud's later instinct theory, I suggest that this usage differs significantly from what has been understood in general psychoanalytic parlance.

This different concept of motivation, viewing interaction of subject and object as the creator of motivational processes, and assuming a basically adaptive and cooperative, rather than intrinsically antagonistic, relationship of infant and environment is key to understanding Loewald's view of therapeutic action. He writes, "Pleasure and unpleasure, at this [infantile] stage, are global states of being. And an adequately empathic mother is, as a matter of fact, a participant in this stage of being, no less or hardly less than the infant" (1971a, p. 134).

Interestingly, Loewald wrote his paper on therapeutic action while the core ideas of that paper were far from accepted in the psychoanalytic community and had hardly been developed in his own work. Many of his key papers (e.g., "On Internalization" [1973], "On Motivation and Instinct Theory" [1971a], "The Transference Neurosis: Comments on the Concept and the Phenomenon" [1971b], and two papers on the superego in 1962) were written after "On the Therapeutic Action of Psychoanalysis." One of the intellectual mysteries of this extraordinary paper is the source for Loewald's vision of the nature of psychic life and for the power of his conviction about his ideas. Although similar ideas were "in the analytic air" and other analysts were criticizing aspects of traditional theory during the '50s (Rado and Horney had already split from the New York Psychoanalytic Institute), this paper seems a good example of how intuitive understanding precedes detailed knowledge of processes, a common occurrence in the history of science. More effectively than anyone else, Loewald was able to create a living, humanistic description of an adaptational mode of psychoanalytic action. Interestingly, neither Rado and his group, nor the English analysts, nor Sullivan, Horney, and others who were part of the profound critique of traditional libido theory are mentioned in the bibliography of Loewald's 1960 paper. The relevant work of the infant researchers had only just begun, and the critical findings of Stern (1985) and others were not available. However, this alternate view of psychoanalysis as a nonmechanistic, open-ended, and personal-agency-centered activity was part of the intellectual ferment of the time and the source of bitter disputes. Loewald was one of the few with the philosophical background, humanistic outlook, and personal qualities that would enable him to see ahead as clearly and courageously as he did. However, Loewald, too, experienced the deaf ear that was then generally turned to what is now an accepted, perhaps even the prevailing view of mental life held within the psychoanalytic community. In 1970, writing in his nonmetapsychologic mode, he said, "To discover truth about the patient is always discovering it with him and for him as well as for ourselves and about ourselves. And it is discovering truth between each other, as the truth of human beings is revealed in their interrelatedness. While this may sound unfamiliar and perhaps too fanciful, it is only an elaboration, in nontechnical terms, of Freud's deepest thoughts about the transference neurosis and its significance in analysis" (pp. 297–298). "In many quarters there still seems to be a tendency to put up a 'no admittance' sign where metapsychological considerations point to object relations as being not merely regulative but essential constitutive factors in psychic structure formation" (p. 299).

At the risk of great oversimplification I will summarize some of those ideas that constitute the basis for his paper on therapeutic action, as well as for the thrust of Loewald's life work.

1. Loewald is dedicated to the idea of the centrality of interactional processes in every aspect of human existence. He, like Sullivan, is unable to conceive of the individual except in the matrix of his interactions. Mental life begins with interactions, not with instincts.

2. This leads him to a conviction of the constitutive nature of object relations, viewed as the internalization of the interactional processes of the individual with its objects, not internalization of the object itself: ". . . the primary datum for a genetic, psychoanalytic psychology would be object relations. This relatedness is the psychic matrix out of which intrapsychic instincts and ego, and extrapsychic objects, differentiate" (1978c, p. 216). External reality, no less than "inner" reality, is the result of the hierarchic organization that is achieved by internalization.

3. The real environment within which the infant is achieving its psychic organization is really important. Loewald believes as strongly as Kohut ever did that the empathic milieu of the child during development and of the analyst during analysis are the vital ingredients for the development of psychic health.

4. Loewald emphasizes the achievement, through structure-building, of increasingly complex, inclusive, preconsciously available organizations of instinctual and environmental stimuli (1973). In contrast to the position of more traditional ego psychologists, defense and compromise formation are downplayed, almost but not quite regarded as forms of psychopathology, while hierarchical organization with permeable boundaries between unconscious and preconscious and between internal and external allows for constant change and continued growth. Pathology, for Loewald, is the imposition of secondary process for the purpose of maintaining primary process ideation, isolated and unaffected by reality. In normality there is a continuing transformation of primary process activities into preconscious language-available processes and continuing interplay between them. Growth and change never cease. The intensity and richness of life derive from the constant refreshment of consciousness from primary process sources.

5. Loewald is at one with Strachey in believing that psychoanalysis is a treatment in which the process of normal development is resumed, with the analyst in the role of a better parent. Some undefined "core" in the individual, called instinct as easily as anything else (although Rado called it the action-self and Kohut chose to call it the self), leads the infant through its interactions with its environment to differentiate into a unique individual.

How does treatment work in this model? Loewald's description is subtle and many-faceted, but I will mention only two aspects of the mode of therapeutic action, both stressed by Loewald in his landmark paper on therapeutic action.

Loewald gives this summary of his view of *the goals* of therapeutic action:

> . . . ego development, arrested or distorted in neurosis, is resumed in analysis. The analyst helps to revive the repressed unconscious of the patient by his recognition of it; through interpretation of transference and resistance, through the recovery of memories and through reconstruction, the patient's unconscious activity is led into preconscious organization. The analyst, in the analytic situation, offers himself to the patient as a contemporary object. As such he revives the ghosts of the unconscious for the patient by fostering the transference neurosis, which comes about in the same way in which the dream comes about: through the mutual attraction of unconscious and "recent," "day-residue" elements. Dream interpretation and interpretation of transference have this function in common: They both attempt to reestablish the lost connections, the buried interplay, between the unconscious and the preconscious. [1960, p. 249]

This description represents an ego psychological advance over the position taken by Strachey, updated but not in itself very startling. But there is another side to Loewald, to me the more exciting one, that emerges when he describes how this goal is achieved by the psychoanalytic *process*. In discussing the patient–analyst relationship and Freud's insistence on the scientific nature of the treatment process, he says, ". . . I believe it to be necessary and timely to question the assumption, handed to us from the nineteenth century, that the scientific approach to the world and the self represents a higher and more mature evolutionary stage of man than the religious way of life" (p. 228).

It is this alternate philosophy that informs his view of therapeutic action. He switches both language and perspective when he says that an analyst requires an objectivity and neutrality the essence of which is love and respect for the individual and for individual development. This love and respect represent that counterpart in "reality," in interaction with which the organization and reorganization of ego and psychic apparatus take place.

The parent–child relationship can serve as a model here. The parent ideally is in an empathic relationship of understanding the child's particular stage in development, yet ahead in his vision of the child's future and mediating this vision to the child in his dealing with him. This vision, informed by the parent's own experience and knowledge of growth and future, is, ideally, a more articulate and more integrated version of the core of being that the child presents to the parent. This "more" that the parent sees and knows, he mediates to the child so that the child in identification with it can grow. The child, by internalizing aspects of the parent, also internalizes the parent's image of the child—an image that is mediated to the child in the thousand different ways of being handled, bodily and emotionally. . . . The bodily handling of and concern with the child, the manner in which the child is fed, touched, cleaned, the way it is looked at, talked to, called by name, recognized, and rerecognized—all these and many other ways of communicating with the child, and communicating with him his identity, sameness, unity, and individuality, shape and mold him so that he can begin to identify himself, to feel and recognize himself as one and as separate from others yet with others. . . .

In analysis, if it is to be a process leading to structural changes, interactions of a comparable nature have to take place. [1960, pp. 229–230]

This is the language of human interaction, far from metapsychology. It is of a piece with this view that interpretations are referred to as forms of poetry expressing the ineffable—a far cry from the idea of exact interpretation that occupied Strachey.

The analyst works by being an emotionally related object, with an important gradient of organizational maturity between him and his patient, mindful of the patient's core of potential being, which he senses as a parent does, oriented toward the future, offering the patient opportunities to create new integrations on the armature of maturity that the analyst provides. His task is empathic communication, uncovering, and guidance toward a new synthesis. This phenomenologic, interactive description of the *role* of the analyst is qualitatively different from Loewald's metapsychological description of the *goals* of analysis that I quoted earlier. This description places therapy in a different universe from that dreamed of by Strachey, or even by Fenichel. Sullivan and Rado were interested in similar models, but they were too attached to positivist science to be able to develop them. Hartmann began with a similar vision but quickly abandoned it. The English analysts, such as Winnicott and Fairbairn, are closest to Loewald, and of course, Kohut, stripped of his special metapsychology, is very near to sharing this outlook.

At the present time, these two descriptions of analytic activity, the metapsychological description of goals, and the interactive and phenomenological description of process, are not readily translatable into each other; they are parallel rather than integrated. The discrepancy of two languages and two points of view continues throughout Loewald's work. Unfortunately, no metapsychological description will yield the prescription that Loewald gives for carrying on psychoanalytic work, although bad metapsychology can inhibit or prevent such work as Loewald recommends. It is a major task of psychoanalysis today to unify these two forms of description. This remains the "cutting edge" of the development of psychoanalysis. Without such unification we lack scientific guidance in the conduct of our clinical work. We are forever indebted to Loewald for giving us both of these descriptions of the nature of therapeutic action and for stirring us to continue to explore the interactive world he outlined.

Chapter Four

Internalizing
Loewald

ROY SCHAFER, Ph.D.

Among the writers of note in the recent history of psychoanalysis, few have a voice that we feel immediately to be distinctive. Loewald is one of these. Winnicott, Erikson, and Kohut are others. Being a distinctive voice, it does not allow us to pick over its utterances casually or to center on just one or another of them, thereby to elude the speaker himself. Loewald resists appropriation through reductive synopsis of the content of his remarks. Although the voice is consistently meditative and modest, it does what any distinctive voice does: It seems to insist on speaking through us. As we continue to listen, we become engaged in the process that Loewald has returned to again and again—the process of internalization. Further, and as a direct developmental consequence of internalization, we become engaged in the unending process of emancipation from internalized authority. Consequently, preparing this discussion has been for me a further extension of my continuing processes of internalizing and emancipating myself from Loewald. These are processes that began and were intensified long ago: in the mid-1950s, when he supervised my first analytic case, and again in the mid-1960s, when I assisted him in organizing a study group on—guess what?—internalization.

"On the Therapeutic Action of Psychoanalysis" offers too much to deal with all of it adequately in a brief discussion. And for the reasons I just gave, focusing on its content is an act that has to combine submission and rebellion. I shall dwell on two of its components: the evocative idea of the analyst as a new object, which I want to elaborate, and the (for me) problematic status of Loewald's adherence to Freud's most abstract metapsychological concepts (for example, eros).

THE ANALYST AS NEW OBJECT

In one way, Loewald's thesis of the analyst as new object is not difficult to grasp and accept—especially not these days, 30 years and several analytic generations after he ventured to submit it for publication. The thesis comprises a number of ideas, which I shall now summarize.

When analysis is effective, it frees the analysand to develop toward levels of integration higher than those reached so far. This development occurs in the field of the analytic relationship. The primary and forever influential precursor of the analytic field is the field of the mother–infant relationship where development necessarily and fatefully originates. In both fields, the mother first and later the analyst represent to the patient a higher level of being, relating, and mutual definition of selves. They hold out their higher level and create a tension relative to the child's/patient's more primitive levels, and in this way give direction and focus to developmental strivings. They make of these relationships growth fields. Consequently, the child-turned-analysand, who is now growing as never before, enters into new modes of relationship with another person, the analyst. These are modes that the patient has not yet conceived, attempted, maintained, or integrated. A new kind of relatedness is now felt to be not only possible but also necessary, safe, and gratifying. On this basis we can say that a new kind of significant object has come into existence. Along with that new object, there has come a new self that in significant measure continues to reflect that new object's perceptions.

The analyst is a new object also in offering a special pattern of interests, capacities, functions, ideas, and emotional experiences to assist this growth process. Included here is the analyst's capacity to partially regress to the analysand's response level, when and where indicated, to help free, through understanding, empathy, and interpretation, the analysand's growth potential. Here Loewald steadily draws parallels to—without advocating or even suggesting the possibility of literal copies of or replacements for—the infant's mother. And in this connection especially, one gets a clear view of Loewald's consistent and brilliant attention to preoedipal phases of development.

Looked at historically, these were bold propositions to set forth to the ultraconservative Freudian audience that prevailed in the United States around 1960. Contained in the idea of the analyst as a new object were a number of significant modifications of the then-received Freudian structure- and function-oriented theory of psychological development and neurotic psychopathology. Loewald was putting forward an interpersonal and experiential field theory in which drives, for example, were to be regarded as products of differentiation within this field rather than primary forces that seek out objects to discharge themselves on or through; thinking quite differently, conservative theorists continued to describe drives as bringing structures and relationships into being where none had existed.

Loewald's precursors and contemporaries in this connection include—more or less closely—Sullivan, Fairbairn, Erikson, Winnicott, Kardiner, and Heinz Hartmann (in his work on adaptation specifically). In Loewald's presentations, drives are no longer where we begin; they are something between a mode of experience and a developmental achievement, though they retain their propulsive role. Meanwhile, Freud's reflex-arc model of drive stimulation and discharge is challenged, for human beings or the selves of human beings emerge as social and interactive from the first. Additionally, the analytic patient is to be viewed primarily from the vantage point of arrested development, interpersonally and experientially, and not, as Freud usually suggested, as a developed tripartite mental structure with focal areas of fixation and regression (although in his own way Loewald has retained the tripartite structural model). It is only within this radically revised context of theory that we can fully appreciate the idea of the analyst as a new object; the easily accepted, commonsense view of a new object—accepting, giving, empathic, and not much else—does not do justice to Loewald's contribution.

To carry these ideas further, let us look at Loewald's occasional and mostly unelaborated references to "analytic love" or the analyst's "love" for the patient. Surely, "analytic love" as one aspect of the analyst as a new object is a daring idea to utter in Freudian company, and surely it remains in need of further explication, as Loewald never really spelled it out. By "analytic love" Loewald does not mean heightened countertransference in the usual sense, although, as he makes plain in his discussion of transference, he would be the first to say that this love includes transference in relation to the patient. Analytic love includes transference in the same way that, for him, every relationship presupposes or requires transference. Nor would he rule out some heightening of countertransference in connection with the analyst's facilitative and technically less constrained regressions and identifications with the analysand, especially when working in the context of preoedipal issues. I believe, however, that Loewald is aiming at something more than these factors when he speaks of analytic love. He approaches his meaning when he speaks, for example, of holding in trust the ego core or potential self of the analysand through all the trials of analysis, and also when he speaks of the analyst seeing the patient as more than he or she can yet conceive and thereby taking on the responsibility of safeguarding a future for that person.

What gets at Loewald's meaning best is, I think, a discussion by the poet Rilke (1907). In a letter to his wife, Rilke was describing his efforts to comprehend the artist Cézanne at work. Cézanne's paintings had just burst on his consciousness in a way that made him feel that "I must change my life." Before going further, I should say that I suppose that Rilke was writing about his own artistic aspirations as well as Cézanne's way of working; I further suppose that he was also doing a piece of creative writing about love as well as about artistic creativity in general. I make these assumptions to indicate my belief that there is no one right and unambiguous way of delivering Loewald's meaning, or Rilke's meaning, or anyone else's meaning, although whatever the context of aims and methods, usually there are some ways that seem to serve a whole lot better than others. Here now is Rilke, in a translation by Joel Agee:

> You also notice, a little more clearly each time, how necessary it was [for Cézanne] to go beyond love, too; it's natural, after all, to love each of these things as one makes it: but if one shows this [love], one makes it less well; one *judges* it instead of *saying* it. One ceases to be impartial; and the very best— love—stays outside the work, does not enter it, is left aside, untranslated: that's how the painting of sentiments came

about. . . . They'd paint: I love this here; instead of painting: here it is. In which case everyone must see for himself whether or not I loved it. This [love] is not shown at all, and some would even insist that love has nothing to do with it. It's that thoroughly exhausted in the action of making, there is no residue. It may be that this emptying out of love in anonymous work, which produces such pure things, was never achieved as completely as in the work of this old man. . . . [pp. 50–51; Rilke's italics]

Here now is Loewald (1970) speaking along strikingly similar lines:

Scientific detachment in its genuine form, far from excluding love, is based on it. In our work it can truly be said that in our best moments of dispassionate and objective analyzing we love our object, the patient, more than at any other time and are compassionate with his whole being.

In our field scientific spirit and care for the object . . . flow from the same source. It is impossible to love the truth of psychic reality, to be moved by this love as Freud was in his life work and not to love and care for the object whose truth we want to discover. All great scientists are moved by this passion. Our object, being what it is, is the other in ourselves and oneself in the other. To discover truth about the patient is always discovering it with him and for him as well as for ourselves and about ourselves. And it is discovering truth between each other as the truth of human beings in their interrelatedness. [pp. 297–298]

Loewald's thesis here is stunning and bold. But consider in addition the following facts: (1) Here, he invokes science so pointedly; (2) in another paper (1975, pp. 352–371), on the analogy between analysis and theater, he casts the analyst in the role of director; and (3) he omits references to analytic love in the index of his book. May one not think that this changing emphasis bespeaks some uneasiness on Loewald's part, uneasiness about departing too far from the model of Freud, the detached scientist? Might it not point to another and thornier aspect of Loewald's project?

LOEWALD'S ADHERENCE TO FREUD'S METAPSYCHOLOGICAL CONCEPTS

Increasingly, while listening to Loewald over the years, my impression has become more distinct that, far more than with anyone else, he has been in a continuing dialogue with Freud. There is no question of Loewald's general scholarliness, but his concentration on Freud is remarkable. It is my impression that his attitude in this dialogue has been simultaneously reverential and challenging. Among other things, the *reverence* shows in Loewald's taking Freud's metapsychological concepts, such as eros, thanatos, cathexis, and drive, very seriously and retaining them as frames and armatures for his theoretical thinking. The *challenge* he expresses in this dialogue can be heard in his attempts to revise significantly our understanding of what these metapsychological concepts should refer to. I think Freud would have found some of these revisions hard to take.

To formulate Loewald's challenge more broadly, I would say that he has been attempting to work into Freud's metapsychology ideas taken from interpersonal, existential-phenomenological, and field-theoretical sources. In this respect, one sees a family resemblance among Loewald, Sullivan, Erikson, Winnicott, and Kohut. All the while, however, Loewald has shown a greater investment in Freud's most abstract endeavors than any of the others, although he might prefer to say as a serious and first-class revisionist, that he is bringing out the richness of Freud's metatheoretical thinking rather than challenging and revising it—a point to which I shall return later on.

Consider what Loewald has been saying about theory—particularly in the discussions throughout his *Collected Papers* (1980) and not just to those on therapeutic action. As already mentioned, Loewald radically revises Freud's conceptualization of instinctual drives. Also, he redefines primary and secondary process and narcissistic cathexis and object cathexis. He presents all of them as organizing actions of different sorts that are carried out on different levels of development; no longer are they flows and investments of psychic energy that take place in a closed system, and no longer can they be considered outside an interpersonal field. Loewald also reconceptualizes the Oedipus complex so as to give much greater weight to preoedipal development and object relations than Freud ever gave them.

Additionally, Loewald works with a growth principle of innate striving toward higher levels of integration. This principle helps him to understand ordinary personal development as well as the therapeutic action of psychoanalysis. In this connection, although he leans heavily on Freud's late, quasi-biological speculations about eros, not only does he make far more of this concept as an independent psychological force than Freud ever ventured to do, he also makes it into something qualitatively different in that it is now intrinsic to an object relations view of development. No longer is eros a superordinate term for personal striving toward instinctual gratification within a stimulus-reduction, reflex-arc conception of the mental apparatus.

Loewald goes further still. Not only does he question and revise the content of Freud's metapsychology, he also does the same for the epistemological and methodological contexts out of which Freud's concepts issued. All this he does by rejecting Freud's objectivistic, rationalist, and mechanistic principles of knowledge, which were those of nineteenth-century science; in place of these principles he installs the narrative cocreation of analytic data by analyst and analysand as, during the analysis, they shift regressively and progressively over various levels of integration and relatedness. Loewald even throws into question Freud's idealization of the scientific as the highest level of human thought; this he does, for instance, in his occasional and undeveloped critiques of Freud's pejorative handling of religious experience. Throughout, Loewald consistently adheres to his primary interpersonal field model of development and its counterpart in the therapeutic action of psychoanalysis.

What can now be said of Loewald's adhering at the same time to Freud's metapsychological terminology—of his pouring new wine into old bottles and, one might add, leaky bottles at that? He attempts an answer in his later, extended discussion of language in psychoanalysis (1978a). There, on my reading of it, Loewald states his rationale explicitly: The metapsychological terms contain within them a wealth of meanings, only some of which have yet been realized; as we understand more and reflect more, we can derive from them more riches and at the same time enrich them by our explications. Moreover, their metaphoric indefiniteness or ambiguity allows one to work theoretically in a way that is more evocative and unhampered by the constraints of strict definition and rigorous derivation. Thus Loewald not only prefers, but also depends on the poetic possibilities he finds in Freud's mechanistic and organicist theorizing to pursue his own creative endeavors. He cites Freud in support of his own dislike of definitions, although this is the same Freud he feels free to revise, and he does acknowledge that he picks and chooses from Freud. I see this as inconsistency, but perhaps of a kind that is hard to avoid when one is challenging a revered authority with whom one also wants to retain basic ties and identifications.

The result, however, cannot be the strongest of all possible arguments. It is, for example, not a strong argument to treat words in our field as containing anything in their own right. It is retrogressive to proceed as though we are engaged in the exegesis of sacred texts. Our words are best regarded as containing only what we can agree has been put into them, and our agreement should be a function of how these words and others related to them seem to us to have been used by us, by the past and present community of analysts, and by generations of members of the culture in which we live. By historical research and dialogue we may hope to clarify our ideas about what Freud put into these words and even about the state he found them in during his years of study and practice. But it would be to verge on word magic to treasure words as containers of mysteries and, as such, to relish them as occasions for poetic theorizing and in that way to legitimate one's own personal constructions. The realm of theory-making will never lack for ambiguity and turbulence, but these features have to do with competing and ever-evolving approaches to systematization and consensus and not with literariness.

Things appear in a different light when we turn our attention to the poetics of clinical interpretation and clinical commentary. In those contexts, Loewald is, I believe, a master. He shows this mastery, for example, in his memorable discussions of converting ghosts into ancestors through the analysis of transference and also in his discussions of the establishment of the analyst as a new object. But in my view theory requires more precision and stability than that not to slide over into idiosyncratic statement. Adherence to the master's (Freud's) words alone cannot remain unchallenged, for it is not the most fruitful or unconflictedly reverential use of the past, though it is, without doubt, the gentler course to take.

Not so, Loewald might say in response. In effect, he says, "The way I use my intelligence, my imagination, and my experience is Freud's way, and it has its own kind of boldness. It requires a rather poetic conception of theory-making and a closer tie of formal theory to clinical language and subjective experience."

Because Loewald has made a profound contribution to psychoanalysis, there is nothing to be gained from faulting his way of working. But one must try to identify and understand those tensions, inconsistencies, and limitations that tend to dim Loewald's otherwise illuminating work. I conclude with two thoughts about his simultaneous adherence to Freud's metapsychological terminology, which conveys his reverence, *and* his revision of the sense of this terminology, which conveys his challenge. On the one hand, we are witness to Loewald's struggles over his internalization of Freud, where Freud's role is that of the internalized authority from which, according to Loewald, one must be forever emancipating himself even while drawing strength from it. On the other hand, recalling both Rilke on Cézanne's love for the objects he was painting and Loewald on the scientist's love for his object, one can see in Loewald's reworking of Freud's metapsychological concepts a creative expression of love that eventuates in concepts that are indistinguishably Freud's *and* Loewald's. These concepts and their entailments are major and unique achievements in our difficult and changing field.

Chapter Five

On the Therapeutic Action of Loewald's Theory

LAWRENCE FRIEDMAN, M.D.

INTRODUCTION

"On the Therapeutic Action of Psychoanalysis" is something more than a classic paper on treatment. It was the beginning of a major—I believe *the* major—modern explication and enrichment of analytic theory. It demonstrated the theory's strength when doubts were gathering. It showed how analysts could welcome new ideas about human development. It settled the feud between interpersonal and intrapsychic descriptions. It stole a march on the hermeneutic turn in psychoanalysis. Celebrating the lifelong creativity of the personal past, it anticipated much of self psychology and also foreshadowed its stress on empathy. We have reason to marvel at its prophetic ecumenism even before we note that this paper is clearly one of two or three landmarks in the history of the theory of therapeutic action.

The paper became a landmark because it healed a malady of theory. To account for the therapeutic action of Loewald's paper, we must identify what it was that needed curing.

THE PROBLEM

Psychoanalytic treatment seems to be disjointed: It seems to consist of two discordant procedures. On the one hand, analysis is required to mobilize wishes and restart old beginnings. On the other hand, the patient's experience is supposed to take a new turn. It would be nice if treatment gave birth to a new motive that would prompt the new turn, but that doesn't make psychoanalytic sense. So the patient's new turn came to be visualized as a new *process*, distinct from wishing— not a motivated interaction but a carefree play of awareness. Treatment was supposed to move between earthy desire and Platonic love of reality.

Actually, the trouble begins already with the first step, the arousing of desire. For wishes to flourish, there must be both hope and safety. But hopes seem to come from the past and therefore from pathology, while safety seems to require new strength and a new scene. And conversely, newness is frightening, familiarity safe. In either case, safety seems to suffocate innovation. Safety that comes from hopeful, old fantasies leads to old trouble. And if the patient is safe because the treatment procedure ensures that his wishes will fail, then he won't stir.

It had been customary to solve the puzzle by assigning the task of seduction to the analytic *situation* and regarding the analyst himself as a disappointingly safe chaperone. But in the back of his mind the analyst always knew that this was dishonest. He knew that he could not divorce himself from his procedures. He knew that it was *he* (or she) who enticed and endangered the patient. So, clearly, even the first step— the stirring up of wishes—was a task the analyst could neither accept nor avoid.

But what made that equivocation most unsettling was the analyst's awareness that whatever attraction he did exercise was that of a Pied Piper whose plan was to drown the wishes he had attracted in a sea of correction. He was deliberately sponsoring an illusion—making promises he had no intention of keeping. In ordinary life we call that deceit.

The analyst tried in vain to reassure himself that, although he did not give what he seemed to offer, he could make the patient appreciate a more valuable substitute. The formula didn't work: Despite some of Freud's occasional references to the temporary use of suggestion, most analysts (and Freud himself, for instance, in his reply to Jung) did not believe that it was the analyst's job to convert the patient. The analyst is not an educator. Although the patient's path must take a new turn, it must lead to his own goal. If the analyst tried to impose a direction, he would be like anyone else who *wants* something from the patient. In this case he would be someone who wants the patient to trade a personal relationship for understanding. He could then be seen as the current representative of those who had previously exhorted the patient, and would become a familiar figure in the patient's standard drama with but a slightly different accent. And the patient would continue to be wary of the old dangers associated with that figure.

PREVIOUS ANSWERS

A way to avoid this problem is by looking only at one side of the dilemma and building a theory entirely out of the *eliciting* elements of treatment. That is what Ferenczi and Rank (1925) did. In spirit if not in letter, they put aside the double game of first rousing wishes and then dousing them. Instead, they made treatment look like a smooth, straight-line development. They thought that the analyst's interpretation could encourage old hopes while simultaneously reforming them. They minimized the newness of the new turn. They made it seem that once analysis has revived old beginnings, it needs only the light of day to change them. At that point, supposedly, adjustment to reality goes without saying. If this is true, reform can be taken for granted and the analyst can honestly encourage wishes without worrying about being deceitful or seductive.

But the two-step problem is not solved so easily. Strachey (1934, 1937), who wrote the milestone paper before Loewald's, pointed out that reality will not necessarily reform old schemas. The reality we are talking about (for instance, the real analyst) is not a physical reality, visible to all, but a human reality of attitudes and relationships that the patient can elicit less of rather than more, and construe in his own peculiar way. In fact, patients will regularly avoid dangerous explorations of the analyst's real attitude, and they will fit everything they cannot avoid into their old scenario.

How can one get around the patient's restricted access? Strachey's gambit was to watch the patient for the hesitant rumblings of a risky move toward the analyst and then react to it with only so much visible attitude as the patient cannot possibly misconstrue. The patient will not be able to ignore that attitude because he is momentarily worried about what he has just evoked. And he cannot misconstrue it because it is so specific, that is, it does not spread out into a classifiable *relationship* with the patient but deals only with the patient's momentary, passionate provocation.

The analyst's narrow response shows that he possesses neither weapons nor blessings. He simply finds usefulness in the patient's passion. And he exhibits that surprising attitude just before the patient can disown his approach, so there is no mystery about how the patient is helped to move beyond his fear.

Other writers might say that the analyst is personally nondisclosing, but Strachey indicated that the analyst's reaction shows an attitude, by which I mean that it is evaluative. The analyst is not a complete double-dealer after all: Patients *want* an attitude and they *get* an attitude. Although the attitude is minimal, it has enough definition to be intelligible—even familiar in its species—and so it can be internalized by the patient as a better sort of attitude than the one he customarily takes toward himself. (Strachey described that as introjecting the analyst's superego.)

Strachey was still offering a two-step model: The analyst flashes a fantasy lure, and then turns his coat and surprises the patient by a cool distance. But Strachey brought the two steps a little closer together: The new turn in treatment occurs at least in the same domain as the old lure—it is a development of wishes in a universe of attitudes; it is not a lesson learned from an indifferent analyst about how to forgo old wishes.

Strachey made the transition from one step to the other seem smoother, but something is missing in his account. We are not really told how the analyst can react personally without acting as a particular *sort* of person. After all, the values embedded in even a small personal attitude carry expectations and wishes. Won't an analyst who reveals expectations and wishes be "recognized" as an old figure in the patient's pathological life drama, feared or idealized rather than learned from? We want to be convinced by Strachey, but we find ourselves asking how an analyst can act as the patient's superego without picking up all the childhood meanings of authority? How can the analyst seem to make some acts permissible without becoming the arbiter of what is unthinkable?

This problem was investigated by writers in the '50s and '60s who, we must note, drew regularly on Loewald's work. They tried out several attitudinal formulas that looked promisingly vivid and personal yet safe from misuse by the patient. In the end, even their most generalized attitudes were too identifiably dramatic to sober the patient up, so to speak. Those attitudes let patients believe that they did not have to change but could recruit their analyst to the old wars. Therefore these theorists continued to insist that, following their initial enticements, a second step must introduce interpretations devoid of attitudes. They said: There is an early phase of treatment and a later one, a mother of closeness and a mother of separation, the analyst as physician and the analyst as analyst. While allowing a *motivated* first step of treatment, they still sought the essence of analysis in a second step consisting of *pure propositions* (although that is not what analysts find in other human interactions). But the first step at least shades off into the second rather than seeming to be incommensurate with it.

On reflection, it is apparent that these troubles have to do with the contrast between pattern and change, between past and future. What is needed to solve them is a grasp of the relationship between the parts and process of mind. And the master of that relationship is Hans Loewald. His mastery gave him two keys to unlock the treatment puzzle.

LOEWALD'S TWO KEYS

The most obvious key is Loewald's sensitivity to the process aspect of psychoanalytic theory.

One reason analysts were having difficulty picturing their effect was that they sensed that their significance was restricted by the patient's mental configuration. The analyst either fitted into that configuration or he didn't, so he looked for one congenial part of the apparatus to attach himself to, bargaining as an adversary with other motives. But Loewald knew that *all* structures govern a continuous *process*, and all parts of the mind contribute to that process.

Treatment does not beg entry to the mind as a parasitic process looking for a congenial structure to support it: Loewald set treatment up as an instance of ordinary mental process. He made treatment a part of normal psychology, so he could use all of the balancing perspectives that go into psychoanalytic theory to resolve treatment paradoxes. (He was also able to turn this around and use treatment experiences to resolve paradoxes of theory of the mind.)

Since the whole mind is in continuous process, a wish is not a hidebound insistence but a sustained groping for a new opportunity. The form of an aroused hope is not the end of the hope's story; it is just the raw material for the shape of its success.

In this Piagetian view transference no longer serves as a demonstration of what the patient must grow out of; on the contrary, the patient is attached to the analyst because he can vaguely imagine an unprecedented, differentiated, much more real sort of satisfaction. It is not deceptive for the analyst to foster transference: Everybody is always some sort of transference figure to others. Normally, attachment and passion never cease to bathe the world in (new) meaning. Conversely, petrified wishes are not stiff from self-indulgence, and they don't need shaking to make them grow up. The same act that mobilizes hope also gives it a new turn.

Loewald found his second key in the deep meaning of

"structure." He realized that structure is that which reflects the direction of process. Mental process moves toward higher levels of integration and differentiation. Wishes, thoughts, and perceptions particularize themselves by interacting with more defined meaning systems. In infancy we are shaped by interaction with adults. Then, throughout our lives, this interaction continues within us, our experience growing as we survey our surveying and achieve our achievements. We learn more precisely what we want as we come closer to getting it. Our desires are perfected as we discover new meanings within them. Our pleasures grow as we find ways to make the world satisfy us.

In effect, unorganized motives turn out to be expeditions toward organized opportunities. And these opportunities are discovered both by articulating our motives more finely and by noticing the definition they get from the world's responses.

LOEWALD'S SOLUTION

The year 1960 was an early date to emphasize this dialogic aspect of human experience. Once Loewald had called it to our attention, the analyst's role no longer seemed inescapably illusionist and deceitful. What is most reassuring to the practitioner is Loewald's revelation that even the *difference* between what patients want and what they get is just part of what wanting means—it is already implicit in their wanting from the beginning of life. The analyst's distance hones the patient's wish. If there is no distance there is no reach, and without reach there is no desire. A demanding distance is *part* of fulfillment. One reason why the analyst's new, helpful attitude can be internalized is that an opening was already there for it in the patient's initial attitude. *The patient's quest has all along been a quest for a new turn.* There, at last, we have a straight-line theory of treatment instead of two disjointed steps.

Previously theorists had struggled to make the analyst's reflective activity harmonize with the patient's demanding activity. Reflection and demand seemed at loggerheads. But Loewald said that, in fact, there is reflection in both camps; we filter not just thought but also wishes through progressively more structured forms. The taking up of external structure into internal structure is not limited to one kind of internalization. In general our whole mental process uses the world as we use our inner meaning structures, namely to particularize what is less defined in our living. (The term *ego* refers to that use.) Since this theory shows how the analytic relationship is isomorphic with mental functioning, we begin to see that treatment may have a right to be effective, after all.

But what about the hazards of isomorphism? Don't the patient's internal stereotypes chop up the analytic relationship in a way that unhelpfully reduplicates old experiences? That was, after all, the worry that led analysts to insist on a second step in which the analyst would offer grist for no other mill than his own, chiefly by hiding anything that could be construed as a personal attitude. In that second step of treatment the analyst was supposed to be indifferent; he would just call 'em as he saw 'em. From fear of a parallel between internal and external processes, analysts were forced to assume that patients do not want to change and analysts do not want to influence. And that made it hard to say why anything should happen.

Loewald confronted this fear head-on. As we noted, he argued that patients always want to change. And he went on to declare that analysts always try to influence. Analysts may regard themselves as just observers, but in fact their perceptions during an analytic hour perform a sort of body English. To the treating analyst, the patient is not an illustration of theory. He is more like a discovered value. Now, that sort of knowledge is not just an objective guide that the patient may or may not put to use: It exerts a push or a pull on him. Within the treatment setting, the analyst's knowledge is personal and intentional—one might almost say that it is tendentious, although it is biased only in being a personalized image of the patient's freedom. The patient can in no way escape that propaganda because every different sense he has of himself also is acknowledged and treated as a resource for still greater freedom.

The relationship is thus very close and personal. The analyst is not indifferent. The coherence of his converging interventions shows that he wants something. But it is a something that is satisfied by any role the patient wishes to take or impose, since the analyst can see any role as a token of the freer patient he imagines. And the patient need not fear that experimenting will cost him his stability since, reflected in the analyst's eye, he sees himself already safely taking the risk.

To be in such a relationship with an analyst is to practice the fluid use of one's own resources. That clears up the ambiguity Strachey left about what it is that the patient incorporates from the analyst and why it is that he should care to incorporate it.

THREE OTHER VIRTUES OF LOEWALD'S THEORY

I think all therapists appreciate the phenomenological accuracy of Loewald's description (as would patients if they were familiar with it). That, and its theoretical coherence, are Loewald's most important contributions. But I would like to call admiring attention also to three other beauties of Loewald's theory:

1. Loewald's account finally draws interpretations back into the orbit of the larger treatment scene. Analysts have been timid in theorizing about treatment out of fear that too lush and complex a picture would obscure the role of precise interpretation. Loewald freed theory from that anxiety. To be sure, he draws attention to the presence of personal expectancies in all of the analyst's conduct. And it is true that he compares interpretations to infant handling. But after all, if interpretations are like *nothing* else under the sun, no explanation of their effect can possibly be given. What is important is that, with all the softer interpersonal transactions that Loewald takes account of, he makes it clear that the finest differentiations are performed by precise, verbal descriptions.

2. Loewald has solved a central mystery of all talking treatments: Quite apart from what the analyst does by his interpretations, patients treat themselves by talking *to* an interpreter, that is, by trying to make themselves known to someone they assume can interpret. Loewald tells us why the patient is helped by that very activity. The difference in levels of organization between patient and analyst belongs as much to the patient as to the analyst. By translating his unspoken mind into the language of an imagined understander, the patient is growing himself up. It is the reach and not just the grasp that does the work.

3. One of the measures of Loewald's success is that a picture leaps out of his technical formulas. Technical terms

alone will not do the job. A picture is what is needed. We use technical terms of conflict to discuss how a patient "works." But to say how treatment works we must discuss successful *process*, and descriptions of process are always less specialized than terms of division. The more successful a theory of psychoanalytic action is, the less parochial it will sound. Let me test Loewald's formula for its plain-talk essence:

The analyst's skill frames a virtual image of the patient's potential. Seeing himself reflected that way, the patient learns to savor both his lust and his sensitivity, his memory and his freshness, renewing his most human feature, namely, his reflective freedom. It seems to me that we don't need a bushel of theory to be moved by Loewald's account of the analyst's work.

Chapter Six

Superego and Time

HANS W. LOEWALD, M.D.

EDITOR'S NOTE

"Superego and Time" is a brief chapter that will allow a reader a clear glimpse of some of the factors that make Loewald's approach to psychoanalysis and the mind so unique. He is concerned here with the nature of psychic structure, the term we use to represent our ideas about how the mind is basically organized. Loewald proposes that the structure in psychic structures, the "principle of arrangement," as he puts it, is time, that "psychic structures are temporal in nature." Then he explains that it is not "objective time" to which he refers, but rather to "psychic time."

By confining his field of discourse to psychic reality, Loewald disguises the profundity of his challenge to traditional modes of conceptualization in psychoanalysis. He does not challenge or dispute the necessity or critical importance of objective time and objective reality in human life. But he plainly believes that a psychoanalyst, on the basis of his professional experience and expertise, has little new to say about it. Like anyone else, a psychoanalyst must not deny the truth of objectivity, must often take it into account. But it is psychic reality that is the proper realm for discourse and study, and the only source of data for psychoanalysis. And though he does not shout it, Loewald continually demonstrates that many of the crucial realities of human life may be approached *only* through psychic reality, that so-called objective logic has its own ways of limiting the search for truth, just as subjectivity can. A science of human experience requires a wider frame, a larger context.

The whole concept of psychic structure in psychoanalysis, however, is derived from and retains terminology that is rooted in a worldview that took objective reality, with its positivistic proofs, fixed entities in space, and correlative linear-historical approach to time as bedrock, as a *standard* for truth. The major psychic structures—ego, superego, and id—were therefore initially conceived as analogous to physicalistic, material structures, whose basic building blocks were therefore postulated to be comprised of forces, energies, and atomistic entities. He disagrees that such a model should be a standard of reference for psychoanalysis, for he believes that the data base of psychoanalysis—human experience—cannot be sufficiently encompassed in a frame of reference designed for the comprehension and mastery of material reality. Loewald continues to find the concepts ego, superego, and id valuable—as ways to represent and generalize about significant aspects of human experience. But as he studies the phenomenology of these experiences, what people think and feel, the actual data for psychoanalytic theory, he asserts that a physicalistic model simply cannot do it justice.

As he always does, Loewald emphasizes process and relationship rather than static entities. The notion of "action patterns" replaces that of "states," for example, and it is the *relations* among the "temporal modes" past, present, and future that define psychic time, rather than each being a static concept that can be objectively determined and defined. Past, present, and future are instead conceived of as principles of mental organization.

It is the wide range of Loewald's interests that is highlighted here. His modes of conceptualization are unusual for a psychoanalytic theorist, although many of his ideas would sound familiar to a modern philosopher, historian, literary critic, or theologian. Many fields that have important relations to psychoanalysis, including the natural sciences as well as the arts and humanities, have moved away from the objectivist, positivistic, linear-historical paradigms that dominated Western thought in the late nineteenth century. Some of these models, in setting aside objectivity and predictability as a standard for truth, are often underestimated by classical psychoanalytic theorists.

But a case has often been made in recent years that it may be appropriate for a psychoanalytic theory to represent a worldview. Many have demonstrated that ideologies and values are already strongly implicit in most psychologies. In its essence, psychoanalytic theory tries to get at human nature itself, and many responsible and knowledgeable people—Loewald, I believe, is one of them—have come to the conclusion that human nature simply cannot be fully contained in a model that will only admit of truths that can be falsified by deterministic proofs. Loewald makes it clear how many of the phenomena of our everyday lives and practices will forever elude the constraints of a deterministic scientistic model, but that this need not discourage us. His own approach shows that scholarly, disciplined, and responsible discourse is still possible and that such discourse need not deny the useful findings and techniques of traditional theory and practice. All that is lost is the false certainty implied by a deterministic model.

Other works I would recommend to an interested reader are especially revealing of Loewald's philosophic interests. "Perspectives on Memory" (1976) is a more recent and detailed investigation of what he calls "memorial processes" and their significance in psychoanalysis, with special attention to the psychoanalytic process. *Psychoanalysis and the History of the Individual* (1978) is a series of lectures presented to an audience of nonanalysts that, in nontechnical language, discusses many subjects in relation to psychoanalysis that are traditional philosophic or theological ones, such as man's moral nature and its relation to historicity, transference and its relation to love, and selected aspects of religious experience.

Gerald I. Fogel, M.D.

I am going to present a particular point of view from which I intend to consider the superego. My approach to the problem will thus be one-sided. It is an experiment in thinking and should be taken as such. As I began to concern myself with the theory of the superego, it soon became apparent that this led, among other things, to the problem of psychic structure. What is psychic structure? Physical structures are arrangements in space or, perhaps more accurately, arrangements characterized by spatial relations. What is the principle of arrangement, what is the nature of the relations obtaining in and between psychic structures? We cannot conceive of them as spatial. If we do, we leave psychology and the psychic realm and consider possible physical substrata of psychic structures, not psychic structure as such. The relations between ego and superego, for example, or the relations between various elements within the ego are not spatial relations. Yet they must, insofar as we think in terms of structure and structural relations at all, conform to some principle of arrangement that allows us to conceive of them as structural relations. I suggest that this principle is time, that psychic structures are temporal in nature.

Psychic structures exist in time and develop in time. But I do not speak of time here as a linear continuum of duration or of the sequence of events in physical time-space as observed in objective, external reality. The time concept involved here, psychic time, implies an active relation between the temporal modes past, present, and future. Dynamic mutual relations between psychic past and psychic present are familiar to us in psychoanalysis. From the point of view of objective time, what we call the psychic past, as in transference phenomena, is not "in the past" but in the present; it is active now, yet active as psychic past, it is the actuality of past experiences. The same is true for unconscious memory traces and their relationship to day residues. Both here and in clinical transference phenomena, the psychic past acts on and in the present, it acts on the psychic present and in the objective present. But the psychic present also has an impact on the psychic past; it activates the psychic past. Memory, as recollection, for instance, manifests psychic time as activity; it makes the past present. Anticipation makes the future present. When we speak of object representation, object presentation, drive representation, a concept of time is implied in which "present" is understood as an active process—to present something. To represent or present means to make or keep present, to present, maintain, or re-create presence. Reminiscences, in the sense in which Freud speaks of them when he says that hysterics suffer from reminiscences, pull the psychic present back into some psychic past, although this takes place in the objective present.

Speaking of time in an active sense can be compared to speaking of organization in an active sense. When we call the ego an organization we do not only mean that the ego is a structural unit whose elements are mutually interdependent and interdependent with the whole, not only that it is a system of interdependent functions, but we also have specifically in mind the integrative and differentiating functions of the ego. In other words, the ego is an agency that organizes. It is useful to think of the ego's function of presentation and representation, of creating and re-creating presence, as the temporal aspect of its synthetic or organizing function.

That time plays a prominent part in the structure of the mind as explored by psychoanalysis is, of course, an implicit and explicit tenet of psychoanalytic theory and practice. The study of dreams and neurosis, the importance of infantile development, the phenomena and concepts of regression, fixation, transference, repetition compulsion—to name just these few—make this evident. The temporal modes involved here are past and present. The remarkable fact is that in mental life the past, that is, psychic past, is not in the (objective) past but is active now as past, and that the psychic present acts on the psychic past. The psychic past and the psychic present are represented in psychic systems, agencies, or structures, as Freud has variously called them, which are actual and active in the objective present of mental life. I think it is clear that the system unconscious and, in the later conceptualization, the id are prominently related to what we call the psychic past, although it is by no means clear what the nature of this relation is. It seems to me equally obvious that the system Preconscious–Conscious and, in the later formulation, the ego show prominent relations to the temporal mode psychic present; we need only think, apart from the representational function of the ego, of the connections between the system Pcs–Cs and perception and motility, and of the closeness to the external world and of the reality-oriented functions of the ego. Here again, the nature of such relations to psychic present is obscure. In passing it is worth mentioning that Freud thought there was no need to assume a spatial arrangement of the psychic systems, even though he speaks, by analogy, of the idea of psychic locality, but that it would be sufficient to assume, as he puts it, "that in a given psychical process the excitation passes through the systems in a particular temporal sequence" (*Standard Edition* 5:537). The concept of time involved here is that of objective time, not of psychic, active time; nevertheless, some kind of temporal principle of arrangement is hypothesized.

As I have already indicated, it was my concern with the superego as a psychic structure that led me to such considerations. More specifically, my attention was drawn to the significance of the future, as a temporal mode, for a deeper understanding of the superego, and it was this idea that stimulated the considerations outlined above.

Insofar as the superego is the agency of inner standards, demands, ideals, hopes, and concerns in regard to the ego, the agency of inner rewards and punishments in respect to which the ego experiences contentment or guilt, the superego functions from the viewpoint of a future ego, from the standpoint of the ego's future that is to be reached, is being reached, is being failed or abandoned by the ego. Parental and other authorities, as internalized in the agency of the superego, are related to the child as representatives of a future and of demands, hopes, misgivings, or despair that pertain to an envisaged future of the child. The superego watches, commands, threatens, punishes, forewarns, admonishes, and rewards the ego; it loves and hates the ego. All this we can do with ourselves only insofar as we are ahead of ourselves, looking back at ourselves from a point of reference that is provided by the potentialities we envisage for ourselves or of which we despair. Conscience speaks to us from the viewpoint of an inner future, whether it tells us what we should do or how we should behave in the future, or whether it judges past and present deeds, thoughts, and feelings. Past deeds and thoughts we condemn inasmuch as we have expected more from ourselves, or we approve of them inasmuch as we have lived up to our expectations. Only insofar as we are in advance of ourselves—conceive of ourselves as potentially more, stronger, better, or as less, weaker, worse than we are at present—can we be said to have a superego. That our expectations may be unrealistic, that we may mistake and misjudge our potentialities, is another matter. Conscience, the mouthpiece of the superego, speaks to us, one might say, in the name of the inner future that envisages us as capable or incapable, as willing or unwilling to move toward it and encompass it, just as parents envisaged us in our potentialities and readiness for growth and development. It is possible that the psychoanalytic concept of self as superordinate to the categories id, ego, and superego, when further developed and clarified, may help us to conceptualize these internal relations more precisely.

Freud has used, more or less successively, at times interchangeably the three different terms ideal ego, ego-ideal, and superego. At the risk of doing violence to the fluidity of these terms as used by him, I am going to consider them insofar as they can serve as terms for successive stages in the development toward superego structure. Briefly, the ideal ego represents a recapturing of the original primary-narcissistic, omnipotent perfection of the child by a primitive identification with the omnipotent parental figures. It is an identification representing the reestablishment of an original identity or unity with the environment and would seem to have connotations akin to hallucinatory wish fulfillment. (Just as the early deprivations and disillusionments are undifferentiated antecedents of the later separations and relinquishments, so the early wish-hallucinations are antecedents of the later internalizations and "restitutions of the object in the ego.") This ideal ego represents a return to an original state of perfection, not to be reached in the future but fantasied in the present. This state of perfection of the ego—perhaps the ideal undifferentiated phase where neither id nor ego nor environment are differentiated from one another—gradually becomes something to be wished and reached for. It becomes an ego-ideal, an ideal for the ego, seen in a much more differentiated and elaborated form than previously in parental figures. Perfection now is to be attained by participation in their perfection and omnipotence on the basis of an as yet incomplete distinction between inside and outside, between ego and parental object; it is magical participation. Here a future is envisaged for the ego, but not yet a future *of* the ego. The future state of the ego is to be attained by merging with the magical object. No stable internal structure representative of the ego's self-transcending exists as yet; the self-transcending is dependent on a magical communion with an ideal authority and model taking an intermediate position between external and internal. The ego's future needs to be still embodied externally in order to have any claim on the ego.

We speak of superego, of an inner future of, not merely for, the ego once a share of the oedipal objects is relinquished, once the libidinal-aggressional relationship with the oedipal figures (having gradually developed during the oedipal phase into a relationship with external objects) has been partially given up as an external relationship and has been set up in the ego as an internal relationship; then the ego envisages an inner future of itself, the superego being the representative of the ego's futurity. We know that many people never reach the stage of a reasonably stable superego structure, that the superego as a late structure is peculiarly prone to regressive tendencies in the direction of reexternalization, or on the other hand to a brittle rigidity that permits no further enrichment and growth. For many of us our inner development depends to a large extent on those with whom we surround ourselves to support the weak superego, or we confine ourselves within narrow self-limitations without wider horizons; it is then as though time stands still. The superego as a late structure in mental development shows great variations and fluctuations from individual to individual, as well as in any given individual during his life. As the latest differentiating grade in mental organization it is not only fragile, tending toward dedifferentiation and regression, but also indicating, we may assume, the direction of future human evolution.

Earlier I alluded to the assumption that the temporal mode of the ego, understood as organizing agency, is the present—the present not as a state but as activity, the ego as presence-creating. Similarly, the temporal mode of the superego, the future, is not to be understood as a state but as activity. We cannot do justice, conceptually, to psychic structures unless we conceive of them as systems of action patterns. The relationship between ego and superego, in terms of psychic time, would be a relation between psychic present and psychic future. I shall come back to these relations.

Speaking genetically, the superego is not only a representative of external authorities and models with their demands and expectations, their prohibitions and allurements, but it is also a representative of the id. It is not possible for me to go into the complex connections that seem to exist between the two structural concepts, id and superego. I will emphasize only one aspect: The oedipal introjects, constituting the superego, do not represent strictly realistic external prototypes, but their character is codetermined by the quality and strength of the libidinal and aggressive drives of the Oedipus complex, so that the introjects represent the drives as much as the drive objects. Freud can say, therefore, that "the superego takes up a kind of intermediate position between the id and the external world (*Standard Edition* 23:207). This implies the recognition that the superego is a system, not of intro-jected "objects," but a system of introjections of interactions between id–ego and external world, with the emphasis here on the id aspects of such interactions. In earlier interactions between psychic apparatus and external world, objects and ego become differentiated one from the other; these earlier interactions are the introjections and projections contributing to the formation of the ego (seen from the vantage point of achieved superego formation, they can be recognized as being antecedents or prototypes of superego formation). They do not represent as yet interactions between id–ego and objects but interactions between less differentiated, more fluid sys-tems. The superego, considered as a psychic structure, is, as Freud had clearly seen, a further differentiation of the ego. This further differentiation is brought about by interactions between psychic apparatus and external world that are of a higher order than was possible prior to the relative comple-tion of the organization of the ego and of objects. But it remains a system of internalizations of interactions and not of objects. The interactions that are internalized as superego elements take place between a psychic apparatus definitively differentiated into ego and id, and an external world defini-tively differentiated into distinct objects.

It is clearly the passionate nature of the oedipal object relationships that lets the id loom so large in the nature of the superego. Later modifications of the superego temper this picture if a workable resolution of the Oedipus complex has occurred.

I will only allude here to the relations that must exist between the id and the temporal mode Past. Freud says that one might see the id, "with its inherited trends," as represent-ing the organic past, and the superego as representing "more than anything the cultural past." But since the superego "takes up a kind of intermediate position between the id and the external world, it unites in itself the influences of the present and of the past" (*Standard Edition* 23:206). Freud, however, speaks here of time not as psychic time in the sense in which I tried to delineate it. He speaks, in this same passage, of the external world as representing "the power of the present," meaning "the external world in which the individual finds himself exposed after being detached from his parents" (ibid.). The ego is not mentioned in this connection; nor is the future, except by implication in his quotation from Goethe's *Faust*, which throws some light on the superego: "What thou hast inherited from thy fathers, acquire it to make it thine" (*Standard Edition* 23:207). The id, if it can be said to represent the inherited past, the degree and quality of organization with which we are born, has a future insofar as we make it ours by acquiring it, by imprinting on it the stamp of ego organization. Insofar as this in an unfinished task, and to the extent to which we experience it as an unfinished, never-finished task, our superego is developed. The superego then would represent the past as seen from a future, the id as it is *to be organized*, whereas the ego proper represents the id as organized at present. The three organizational levels—while representing the three temporal modes in a being who has memory, creates presence, and anticipates—coexist as embodied in the three psychic structures, and at the same time are successive. And coexisting, they communicate with each other, define, delimit, and modify each other. A more refined concept of self, as well as a deeper understanding of the phenomenon of consciousness, may help us here.

Considering psychic past and psychic future from a different angle, we can say that the future state of perfection, which is the viewpoint of the superego by which we measure, love and hate, judge ourselves, and deal with ourselves, recaptures the past state of perfection that we are said to remember dimly or carry in us as our heritage and of which we think we see signs and traces in the child's innocence when he is at one with himself and his environment.

I shall now very briefly discuss some aspects of the superego as a psychic structure representing internalizations of oedipal and postoedipal relationships. The superego as a later structure is more fluid, less stable than the ego, although its elements, the superego introjects (owing to the more structured relationship of ego and objects that is the material of these introjections) are more structured than the ego introjects and therefore more easily visible. I suggest viewing the superego as an enduring structure pattern of introjections whose elements may move in the direction of the ego or in the direction of external objects; they may thus lose their character as superego elements and either merge into the ego or regain a measure of object quality; new elements may become part of this structure pattern. This conception implies the notion of degrees of internalization and externalization. Patients reexternalize aspects of their superego by projecting them onto the analyst and internalize aspects of the analyst's personality or, more precisely, of the analyst's relationship with the patient. We frequently hear patients describe the analyst's watchful "presence" in some vague form as the patient engages in given activities in his daily life, showing a certain degree of internalization that does not yet have the quality of being part of the patient's superego. It has more the quality of a fantasy object. In certain hallucinatory experiences of this kind, as most often described by borderline or psychotic patients, externalization has gone a step further, or, seen from the other direction, internalization has not gone as far. A complete relinquishment of the external object relationship has not taken place in these instances. While the superego as a structure pattern is established through the resolution of the Oedipus complex and to the extent to which this resolution has occurred, new elements enter, are assimilated into this structure pattern at various later stages in life, most clearly in adolescence. But they, too, become part of a structure pattern that represents the ego's futurity, and they are selected insofar as they might fit, might be capable of assimilation into this pattern. Superego elements may be given up, expelled; persons in the external world representative of such abandoned elements may be repulsive to the superego, which shows that these elements have left residues in the superego.

Superego elements may merge into the ego as certain goals set for the ego's development have been reached; but the ego, under conditions of stress and ego conflict, may lose hold of them so that they return into the superego structure. Lest the impression arise that I visualize something like peripatetic particles wandering back and forth among ego, superego, and external world, let me emphasize that internalization and externalization are not manipulations perpetrated on passive and static entities, nor movements performed by such entities. The process of internalization or introjection involves a change in the internal organization of the elements; this, while hard to conceptualize, is of the utmost importance. The more clearly the aspects of an object relationship, for instance, between father and son, are internalized, become part of the son's inner world, the more they lose their object-relation character. Another way of attempting to formulate this is to say that internalization involves the process of neutralization. The relationship, being internalized, becomes (relatively) desexualized and deaggressivized. The changing of superego elements into ego elements involves a further desex-

ualization and deaggressivation. The degree of modification
and reorganization of material for introjection that is brought
about by internalization varies with the degree of internalization. In insufficient or in pathological, distorted superego
development the sexual-aggressive character of the internalized element is usually pronounced. Mourning, inasmuch as it
involves the relinquishment and internalization of aspects of
the lost object relationship, leads to an enrichment of the
superego. Such internalization, if observed over long periods
of time, may be progressive so that eventually this superego
element merges into the ego, becomes an ego element, becomes realized as an ego trait rather than being an inner ideal
or command.

In terms of psychic time, the relation between ego and
superego can be seen as a mutual relation between psychic
present and psychic future. In the structure of the superego
the ego confronts itself in the light of its own future. The
establishment of the superego completes the constitution of
an inner world whose dimensions may be said to be the
temporal modes past, present, and future. They have to be
conceived, like anything in the mental realm, as active moves,
not as observed attributes. If we conceive of the superego as a
psychic structure representing the ego's future from the standpoint of which the ego is judged, loved, and hated, the degrees
of internalization, measured by the distance from the ego,
would be steps in the movement from psychic future to
psychic present, as organized in these two structures.

I am aware of the fragmentary and partly speculative
nature of this presentation and of the fact that it raises rather
than solves problems. However, the whole orientation of
psychoanalysis as a genetic approach to mental life, as an
attempt to understand mental disease in terms of the history
of mental development and to cure it by promoting a resump-

tion of this history—using the faculty of remembering as a main tool—points to the importance of time as being somehow the inner fiber of what we call psychical. It seems to me also that, together with the awareness of differentiation of inner and outer and their relatedness, the awareness of differentiation of past, present, and future stands at the threshold of higher mental organization.

Chapter Seven

Psychoanalysis as an Art and the Fantasy Character of the Psychoanalytic Situation

HANS W. LOEWALD, M.D.

EDITOR'S NOTE

Most readers will recognize intuitively and respond positively to many of the phenomena Loewald describes and reasoning he uses to support his conception of psychoanalytic treatment in "Psychoanalysis as an Art and the Fantasy Character of the Psychoanalytic Situation." The art of this chapter disguises, however, the boldness of its reach and the profundity of its arguments.

The central subject is the transference neurosis. There are few concepts in psychoanalysis as controversial as this one. Contemporary theorists argue about its definition, its qualities and characteristics, its usefulness or necessity as a concept, and whether a psychoanalytic process should be defined by it. Some say there is no psychoanalysis if there is no transference neurosis; others claim the concept is a fiction, that the concept of the psychoanalytic process has superseded it. Some go so far as to maintain that when it appears in its classic form, it reflects a major *resistance* to psychoanalysis, one that may reflect a therapeutic stalemate induced by an analyst more interested in his theories than his actual patient. But students learning how to do psychoanalysis still press their teachers and supervisors for how to define and recognize one, and supervisors struggle as well with how to justify and demonstrate the phenomenon.

Although I simplify, I would say that the more classical Freudian analysts, the traditional ego psychologists of today, find the concept viable and useful, while those more influenced by object relations models, including self-psychologists, have tended to move away from it. When referring to intrapsychic events—*mental* events—the representational language of object relations theory is closer to experience, catches more naturally the here and now, the interaction between patient and analyst, which is where the life of an analysis is found. But traditionalists believe that important aspects of the transference neurosis phenomenon are not captured by such an approach.

Where does Loewald fit here? Have no doubt that he believes in the transference neurosis. But his reexamination of the traditional concept throws over much that is traditional about it. In fact, the language he uses would ordinarily be anathema to many analysts who think in traditional categories. Such an analyst might be uncomfortable, for example, to think of important, crucial components of psychoanalysis characterized as *mutual* dramatized reenactments, of *theater* as a major metaphor for the serious business of psychoanalysis, of patient and analyst each using the other *imaginatively*. He probably would also worry at the idea that there are *necessary* and *nonreducible* subtle blends of subjectivity and objectivity, reality and illusion, and fantasy and perception in all good psychoanalytic work. Almost certainly he would balk at the idea of reality testing characterized as a mutual interpenetration and enrichment of fantasy and reality, rather than the replacing or correcting of fantasy *by* reality. He would be concerned about the *dangers* of enactment, the threat to objectivity, the possibilities for suggestion replacing insight, the intimations of play and therefore possible playacting. How can an analyst maintain appropriate technical neutrality, be *responsibly* empathic, not be overinvolved, and maintain

proper control over himself and the analytic situation with
these kinds of things going on? And how can this be reconciled with the classic conception of the transference neurosis?

How Loewald addresses these issues and answers these
questions will be found in this chapter. I have argued else-
where that his papers on the treatment process are the hardest
to summarize. This is because he faces so completely the
actual ambiguities and complexities of analytic work, the interrelations and frequent inseparability in fact among what is
intrapsychic, interpersonal, and intersubjective, and between
subjective and objective, past and present, memory and perception, fantasy and reality. The transference neurosis concept rested for a long time in a theoretical frame that took as
its ideal that of physical science: objectivity and the correla-
tion of historical cause with future effect. Loewald rejects this
as a theoretical frame for the organization of the data of
psychoanalysis, but demonstrates, I believe, that the transference neurosis remains a useful, even crucial concept, because
it has defining characteristics that are unique to analysis, and
these defining characteristics reflect important things about
past, present, and future actualities, about the relationship of
fantasy to reality, the relationship of the patient's unique
individuality to the analytic relationship, and about the realizable potential for authentic insight and analytic change. In so
doing, he does full conceptual justice to the complex, dynamic
realities of intrapsychic and interpersonal process as we actually encounter and conceive them, to the existential and relational realities of all human experience.

Loewald knows how far he has moved from traditional
theory in this chapter, and modestly notes at the outset that he
does not "claim to measure up to the standards of scientific
rigor or conceptual precision." His argument for a wider view
of the relations between science and art and for psychoanalysis's proper relationship to each is brief but persuasive,
however, and I suspect he has no illusion that the phenomena

that he so artfully and comprehensively elucidates for us here could be better accomplished with the tools of scientific method alone. On my reading, the chapter does not lack for conceptual precision in the least.

Readers interested in Loewald's views of the therapeutic process might also look at "Psychoanalytic Theory and the Psychoanalytic Process" (1970) and "The Transference Neurosis: Comments on the Concept and the Phenomenon" (1971b). In fact, almost everything he writes is immediately relevant to clinical analytic process, although he rarely uses clinical material or actually talks directly about analytic technique.

Gerald I. Fogel, M.D.

What follows does not claim to measure up to the standards of scientific rigor or conceptual precision. In the fluidity and ambiguity of thought and style, this presentation is perhaps all too much affected by its subject matter.

Most of us, whether engaged solely in psychoanalytic practice or engaged also in psychoanalytic research and theory-building, stress the scientific aspects and potentialities of our discipline. Freud did so, and he rejected the suggestion that there might be something nonscientific or unscientific, something resembling art, about psychoanalysis. In the recent past there has been much emphasis on psychoanalysis as a basic science or as the foundation for or as part of a general psychology. It has been claimed that this constitutes the lasting value of psychoanalysis, and doubts have been expressed, even within the ranks of psychoanalysts themselves, with regard to its viability as a form of psychotherapy. I myself have no doubt about its therapeutic value and potentialities, although I do question whether we can expect general or ready recognition of its therapeutic worth and effects—given the anti-individualistic tendencies and simplistic behavior-modification trends in our culture.

On the other hand, because of significant shifts and changes in modern understanding of what constitutes truth, in our insight into the relations between reality and fantasy or imagination and between objectivity and subjectivity, we begin to recognize that science and art are not as far apart from one another as Freud and his scientific age liked to assume. Science's dignity is not so readily offended today by the suggestion that both art and science make use of creative imagination. Neither do we take for granted that creative imagination per se is unscientific, nor do we assume that art may not and does not ever employ the stringency of scientific or scientifically informed objectivity.

Thus, in speaking today of psychoanalysis as an art, I neither speak in an antiscientific spirit, nor do I see art as being in opposition to science. Nevertheless, while I see them as closely related, we do distinguish between them. The two words refer to different facets of the human mind's activity.

I

In one sense of art, psychoanalytic *technique* may be called the art of applying psychoanalytic knowledge and the psychoanalytic method to a particular clinical case. Perhaps the latter, the method of investigation and interpretation, may more specifically be called an art (or skill), whereas the body of psychoanalytic observations and theory—the science of psychoanalysis—is made use of in this art. Insofar as investigations and interventions are intended to have a curative effect on the patient's psychic life, psychoanalysis is a therapeutic art.

Considered as a process in which patient and analyst are engaged with each other, psychoanalysis may be seen as art in another sense: The psychoanalytic situation and process involves a reenactment, a dramatization of aspects of the patient's psychic life history, created and staged in conjunction with, and directed by, the analyst. The idea of the transference neurosis expresses this understanding of psychoanalysis as an emotionally experienced recapitulation of the patient's inner life history in crucial aspects of its unfolding. Seen in this light, psychoanalysis shares important features with dramatic art. Aristotle defined tragedy as "the imitation of action in the form of action." Francis Ferguson, in his illuminating book on dramatic art (1949), extended this definition to include drama in all its various forms. The transference neurosis is such an imitation of action in the form of action, or, more correctly, it develops from such imitation in action of an original action sequence and remains under the formative influence of that original action, although in its total development it is uniquely a creature of the psychoanalytic process.

Viewed as a dramatic play, the transference neurosis is a fantasy creation woven from memories and imaginative elaborations of present actuality, the present actuality being the psychoanalytic situation, the relationship of patient and analyst. But in contrast to a play conceived and composed by its author as a deliberate creation of his mind to be enjoyed by an audience, the transference neurosis is an unwitting fantasy creation that is considered or clearly recognized as such—at any rate in earlier stages of the analysis—only by the analyst. The patient often has inklings of it, on his own or intimated by the analyst, even in early stages; but they tend to be swept away and drowned in the poignancy of his immediate experience, to reappear and disappear again and again. But we know that analysis is not feasible without a measure of "observing ego" that can be called upon and gradually strengthened.

The fantasy character of the transference neurosis has been referred to as the make-believe aspect of the psychoanalytic situation. In the promotion and development of the transference neurosis, analyst and patient conspire in the creation of an illusion, a play. The patient takes the lead in furnishing the material and the action of this fantasy creation, while the analyst takes the lead in coalescing, articulating, and explicating the action and in revealing and highlighting it as an illusion (note that the word *illusion* derives from the Latin *ludere*, to play). The patient experiences and acts without knowing at first that he is creating a play. Gradually he becomes more of an author aware of being an author, by virtue of the analyst's interventions that reflect back to the patient what he does and says, and by transference interpretations that reveal the relations between the play and the original action that the play imitates.

As director of the play, the analyst must relive, re-create the action of the play. This he is able to do on the basis of his own inner life experiences and their organization, which are sufficiently similar to those of the patient. While engaging in trial identifications with the patient, that is, with the actors and actions of the play, the analyst is the one to keep an overall view and to direct the actors—not by telling them what to do or how to act, but by bringing out in them what they often manage to express only fleetingly, defensively, haltingly, in inhibited or distorted fashion.

Patient and analyst in a sense are coauthors of the play: The material and the action of the transference neurosis gain structure and organization by the organizing work of the analyst. The author of a dramatic play performs both functions, that is, the function of "imitating" action in the form of action, and the function of giving organization and structure to the material.

The specific impact of a play depends on its being experienced both as actuality and as a fantasy creation. This Janus-face quality is an important ingredient of the analyst's experience in the analytic situation and becomes, if things go well, an important element in the patient's experience. A spectator, if affected by the play in the way I indicated, participates in the action vicariously. But the patient is a direct participant, as well as the initially unwitting coauthor. And the analyst, far from being left to his own devices as spectator by the patient, finds himself cast in the roles of various coactors by the patient, not dissimilar to certain recent staging devices in contemporary theater. But whereas in such modern productions audience participation ordinarily consists in assuming the assigned role, the analyst, instead of assuming that role, reflects back to the patient the role the latter has assigned to him. Thus the transference neurosis again and again is revealed as an imitation of action, a dramatic play having its roots in the memories of original action and deriving its life as a present creation of fantasy from the actuality of the psychoanalytic situation and its interactions. Whenever the analyst engages in mirroring activities and interpretations, the poignant immediacy of the transference neurosis may recede at least momentarily or to some extent without being extinguished, and its character as a fantasy creation stands out in bolder relief: The patient may take some distance from the action.

Parallels between a dramatic play and the transference neurosis could be spun out further, but at this point I wish to qualify some of the things I have said. I stated that the patient tends to be caught up in the poignant immediacy of the transference and the analyst recognizes and reveals its fantasy character. This is not always the case. An obsessive-compulsive patient may have so much distance from himself, may be such a compulsive self-observer or so obsessively entangled in psychoanalytic theory, that he remains or only too promptly reverts to being a detached spectator insisting on the unreality of the transference. It is the analyst who then must take the lead in accentuating and intensifying the patient's experience of the here-and-now immediacy of the transference.

Another qualification: Even though the analyst does not assume the roles assigned to him by the patient in the transference play, the analyst—by telling the patient what the assigned role is, how it relates to the original action, or by demonstrating that the transference has its own actuality—is a participant in an interaction nevertheless. This participation, which is to lead to curative influences on the patient's inner life, constitutes the basis for the transition between the actuality of the transference neurosis as an "artificial illness" (Freud 1914) and the actuality of the patient's life outside the transference neurosis. The analyst's therapeutic art does not consist in mere detached spectatorship and in reporting to the patient what the analyst perceives and how he interprets it, but in the responsive quality of his observations and communications, in the tact and timing of his interventions. It consists in the analyst's capacity and skill of conveying to the patient how he, the analyst, uses his own emotional experiences and resources for understanding the patient and for advancing the patient's access to his, the patient's inner resources. And there may be at times, in addition, that other quality to the analyst's communications, difficult to describe, that mediates another dimension to the patient's experiences,

raising them to a higher, more comprehensively human level
of integration and validity while also signaling the transitory
nature of human experience. The chorus in Greek tragedy,
some soliloquies in Shakespearean plays, or, in a different
way, certain commentaries on the action of the play by Shakespearean fools, for example, may give an idea of this function.

The transition between transference neurosis and the
patient's life outside of it, or the reciprocal communication
between them, is similar to that between a dramatic play, a
fantasy creation, and the life that people lead before seeing the
play and after they come home from an evening in the theater—if the play for them is more than a pastime.

Several questions must be raised at this juncture: What is
the original action sequence that is imitated in the transference neurosis? What is the nature of this imitation? How do
we understand the term *transference neurosis*? What of those
aspects of the psychoanalytic situation and process that are
not dramatic reenactments of the past? Finally, we cannot
avoid the difficult but crucial issue of the presumed antithesis
of fantasy and reality.

The original action imitated by the transference neurosis
would be the so-called infantile neurosis. In the traditional
view, the nucleus of the infantile neurosis is the Oedipus
complex and its conflicts. Some recent papers (e.g., Blos
1973, Tolpin 1975) stress a distinction between the infantile
neurosis as an actual childhood illness caused by oedipal
conflicts and characterized by given symptoms, and infantile
neurosis as a term for the pathogenic oedipal conflict situation itself or for its reconstruction from the transference
neurosis. This distinction is of theoretical and practical importance. But relevant in our present context is the central
position of the Oedipus complex in either case. While there is
no doubt that the Oedipus complex occupies a central posi-

tion in psychic development, there is today general agreement that preoedipal developmental issues are of far greater pathogenic import than the older view of neurosis assumed or allowed for. And I am thinking here not of psychotic or borderline conditions, or even of the so-called narcissistic character disorders, but of those conditions that are characterized either as symptom neuroses or as character neuroses. I would therefore include pathogenic and pathological preoedipal disturbances and deficiencies as relevant for infantile neurosis and transference neurosis (cf. Ritvo 1974).

We have also come to recognize more explicitly that the transference neurosis is not simply an imitation or resumption of infantile oedipal conflicts or of their pathological resolution, but that it is strongly influenced in the majority of cases by the reworking and revisions of such problems during adolescence. I am thus taking the liberty of expanding the term *transference neurosis* to include also the imitation of adolescent action.

So far I have discussed two of the questions I raised: What is the original action that is imitated in the transference neurosis? and How is the term *transference neurosis* to be understood here? Let me add that each later stage in development—later, that is, than the early preoedipal stages—may be understood as a resumption on a higher level of fundamental issues of psychic development. Psychic development takes place in interaction with environment. The transference neurosis itself also represents such a resumption.

This last consideration leads to the question: If we characterize the transference neurosis, in thinking of it as dramatization, as an imitation of action, what, then, is the nature of such imitation? No drama or play is an imitation of action in the sense of copying the original action, or even of involving only a degree of selection and highlighting of certain events in an action, as is the case in a documentary or newsreel. The imitation of action represented by a play is a reenactment that understands and implicitly reinterprets an action from certain points of view and in certain directions that are strongly influenced by the present actuality of the author, including the *Zeitgeist* of his epoch, and, when it comes to performance of the play, by the present actuality of directors, actors, and audience. In the tragedies of *Oedipus Rex* and *Antigone*, for example, the original action itself—not unlike the original action of the transference neurosis—is shrouded in the fogs and ambiguities of history and myth. It is transmitted to Sophocles already laden with beliefs, biases, distortions, and interpretations on the part of the generations that stand between him and the original action. Whatever he conceived of as the original action he then reorganized and reinterpreted according to his lights and those of his time. Modern dramatizations of the same theme, modern imitations of the same action reorganize and reinterpret that same theme, which meanwhile has gained new layers of understanding and misunderstanding; these are apt to have become part of what is conceived of as the original action (comparison with screen memories suggests itself). Indeed, it may now be Sophocles' tragedy that is taken as the original action to be imitated.

For analysts, not long ago it was the Oedipus complex or the failures in resolving it that represented the original action imitated in the transference neurosis. When Freud called it the Oedipus complex, he gave that name to an infantile conflict situation on the basis of his own interpretation of the Oedipus story. He also determined for a generation of analysts and others what was to be conceived as the original action to be resolved and reworked in later life, and how it was to be understood. By now the Oedipus complex itself tends to be seen as a reworking, as a reenactment on a higher developmental level of early infantile stages of psychic development, which latter are assuming the status of "the original action."

From the vantage point of the transference neurosis it seems best, at least provisionally, to consider as the original action the conglomerate of preoedipal, oedipal, and adolescent action sequences. These are being imitated in the transference actions. The analyst's insights into the historical nature and layering of the patient's symptoms, character traits, of his inner life story make it possible to view his various actions in the analytic situation as transference actions, as imitations of earlier actions.

At this point it seems indicated to drop the term *imitation* (which we had adopted for purposes of exposition from Aristotle's definition of tragedy) and to substitute for it the terms *reenactment* and *repetition*. Repetition as a term has its own ambiguities, but it is more familiar to us in discussions on transference and memory. When Freud distinguished between repetition and recollection, he characterized repetition as reproduction in action, reenactment (1914). In the course of the development of the transference neurosis, transference actions are revealed (interpreted) as a form of memory. As they are revealed as repetitions of earlier action, they gradually acquire the character of so-called make-believe, or better, of fantasy play, when viewed from the standpoint of present actuality. Present actuality and past actuality become clearly distinguishable or differentiated for the patient—insofar as his transference actions and reactions are concerned—only through the common analytic work, that is, by virtue of the interactions of patient and analyst in the analytic situation. The patient's recognition of the fantasy aspect of the analytic situation cannot be taken for granted in earlier stages of the analysis. When it comes to the transference repetitions, it is as though the differentiation of past and present—one of the crucial advances in early psychic development—has to be undertaken all over again. We know that this differentiation tends to recede in proportion to the increasing intensity of affect even in recollective remembering.

I have pointed out that the "imitation of action in the form of action," represented by a dramatic play, is not a copy of the original action. Such imitation or, as we term it now, such repetition in the form of reenactment, consciously and/or unconsciously reorganizes and reinterprets original action from certain points of view and in certain directions that are strongly influenced by present actuality. Applied to the transference neurosis, this means that the patient's presenting illness or emotional disorder, his present life circumstances, expectations, and frustrations, and in particular also the various facets and rules of the analytic situation and of the individual analyst all influence the reenactment of past experience represented by the transference neurosis. Furthermore, the reexperience by reenactment of the past—the unconscious organization of the past implied in repetition—undergoes changes during the course of treatment. In good part these changes depend on the impact of current experiences with the analyst that do not fit the anticipatory set the patient brings to his experiencing another, mainly parental, person. In this manner the way of reliving the past is apt to be influenced by novel present experience; certain past experiences are seen in a different light and felt differently. Inasmuch as reenactment is a form of remembering, memories may change under the impact of present experience. Influenced by the analyst's nonreactive response to the patient's assigning him the role of a castrating father, for example, the patient may for the first time reenact more positive interactions with his father in the transference and may bring up recollections of his father of a positive nature. It is thus not only true that the present is influenced by the past, but also that the past—as a living force within the patient—is influenced by the present.

Parenthetically, a word should be said here about the so-called corrective emotional experience. The novel experiences with the analyst in the psychoanalytic situation that I have mentioned have nothing to do with role-playing on the part of the analyst, much less with the analyst's taking a role opposite to the one assigned to him by the patient—connotations that the expression carries with it ever since Franz Alexander used it years ago. Without going into detail here, I wish to point out that it is the very fact of the analyst's ability to show the patient the role the latter has assigned to him and the genesis of this assignment—it is this empathic objectivity of the analyst, perceived by the patient, that carries the potentiality for change. It is neither insight in the abstract, nor any special display of a benevolent or warm attitude on the part of the analyst. What seems to be of essential importance is insight or self-understanding as conveyed, as mediated by the analyst's empathic understanding, objectively stated in articulate and open language. This activity of the analyst has nothing whatever in common with role-playing. If defenses do not interfere, it is experienced by patient and analyst alike as authentic responsiveness. This responsiveness *is* an essential element in what we call emotional insight because it frees the patient for nondefensive responses of his own. Interpretations of this kind explicate for the patient what he then discovers to have always known somehow, but in the absence of its recognition and explication by the analyst such knowledge could not be grasped and acknowledged.

The foregoing discussions underline the complexities of the dramatic reenactment and the changes and shifts occur-

ring in the course of the transference neurosis and its gradual
resolution. But I have so far said little about the fantasy
character of the transference illness. This fantasy character is
apparent to the patient if and when he distinguishes between
the past and the present and between his own inner experience of the moment and the overall context of his life in
which the analysis takes place. These two distinctions are
intimately related, but I shall concentrate now on the latter.
There are again parallels between the analytic situation and
the situation of the various participants (including the spectator) in the performance of a play. The deeper the spectator
gets absorbed in the action of the play, for instance, the more
does he lose his overall perspective on himself as a person
who has gone to the theater for a certain purpose and in a
certain frame of mind or mood. The actors become even
more identified with the play's action and personages. So do
the author and the director during certain phases of their
work.

In the course of an analysis as a truly meaningful experience in the patient's life, the regressive pull of the analytic
situation is more or less counterbalanced or repeatedly cor-
rected by the patient's life outside that situation. True, his
outside life is influenced and troubled by regressive tendencies that have led him to seek treatment. But he functions
there, to some extent at least, within the context of his present
life actuality. Insofar as he has come to the analyst for help,
having decided that he needs and wants help of this sort,
having inquired who might be suitable and available, having
made the various necessary arrangements involved and more
or less adhering to them throughout the analysis—doing all
this, the patient manages to function within the context of
present actuality in regard to the analytic situation, too. It is
principally during the analytic hour itself that this other actu-

ality, the actuality of his fantasy life, of memories of the past, is mobilized and tends to take over.

The fantasy character of the psychoanalytic situation, the transference-neurosis aspect of that situation, is apparent to the patient at those times when he is able to juxtapose it with his present actuality, and in particular with the analytic situation in the context of his present life actuality. The clearest example is the patient with a gift for histrionic dramatization who now and then, emerging from the unmitigated expressions of his infantile wishes and frustrations in the transference, regains his perspective as an adult. As that adult he knows that he has come to another adult for help, hoping or trusting that the analyst is more experienced, more knowledgeable, and more mature in regard to emotional life than he himself. As an adult the patient also knows that he is not altogether the child he makes himself out to be, or the child he lets take over in the regressive pull of the analytic situation. For other types of patients, as indicated earlier, the problem is not their easy yielding to the regressive pull, but their clinging to the rationality of present levels of ego organization. Nevertheless, if the analysis progresses, infantile fantasy levels will be significantly experienced so that the necessary juxtaposition between transference neurosis and present actuality can take place.

Fantasy here does not mean that something takes place that is not to be taken seriously or that is unreal. Patients, when they emerge from an analytic hour where their infantile life took over, often think so, as they tend to think in regard to dreams. While analysts are more sophisticated about dreams and fantasy life, they all too frequently fall into the error of regarding fantasy as being opposed to reality, as something to be eventually discarded or relegated to a psychic enclave. But fantasy is unreal only insofar as its communication with present actuality is inhibited or severed. To that extent, however, present actuality is unreal, too. Perhaps a better word than *unreal* is *meaningless*. In the analytic process the infantile fantasies and memories, by being linked up with the present actuality of the analytic situation and the analyst, regain meaning and may be reinserted within the stream of the total mental life. Thereby they may resume that growth process (an element of which we call sublimation) that was interrupted or interfered with at an earlier time, leading to neurosis. At the same time, as the present actuality of the analytic situation is being linked up with infantile fantasies, this present gains or regains meaning, that is, that depth of experience that comes about by its live communication with the infantile roots of experience. The disruption of that communication is the most important aspect of the problem of defense, of repression, isolation, and so on.

We know that the further back we go from adult psychic life into infantile life, the less are fantasy and reality antithetical. The 2-year-old, for example, hardly distinguishes between dream and actual life occurrences. The distinction between confabulation and objective truth has little or no meaning for him. In later childhood the child appears to distinguish between his play world and other aspects of his world, or between his play activities and his other less fanciful and more sober activities. But these two different worlds and activities each have their own dignity as something real for him. The two realities coexist and communicate with and influence each other. For the adult there is far greater separation between these two worlds. If communication between them is disrupted we have each in its own corner: a conscious and/or unconscious fantasy life that proliferates on its own (a kind of malignant growth), and opposed to it what we call objective reality, which tends to lose meaning as it seems to gain in objective rationality. This is a caricature of ego and id in irreconcilable opposition. In the healthier adult, communication and interplay between the world of fantasy and the world of objectivity, between imagination and rationality, remain alive. He is aware that play or drama and actual life share reality, that one gains meaning from the other, and that a great play may tap deeper sources of reality and meaning than the sober rationality of the workaday world alone can call forth.

Psychoanalysis in its scientific approach to psychological problems, that is, in acknowledging and exploring the unconscious, and especially also as a psychotherapeutic art, has greatly contributed to revitalizing the communication and interplay between fantasy and rationality. In many of its conceptualizations psychoanalysis, nonetheless, is still affected by the disease of the age and especially of official science—the disruption between fantasy and rationality—that it is intended to cure or ameliorate. I have no question that Freud was conscious of attempting to do more than heal neuroses of individuals. In fact, this latter purpose of psychoanalysis seemed more and more to take second place in his interests. That he and his friends spoke of psychoanalysis not only as a science and as a form of psychotherapy but also as the psychoanalytic *movement*, that they were concerned with anthropology, mythology, and civilization and its discontents—all this shows that they had larger aims and vistas, namely to influence and change the outlook and behavior of a whole era in regard to the relationship and balance between rational and instinctual life and between fantasy and objective reality.

But Freud does not appear to have recognized that the objective reality of science is itself a form of reality organized (although not created in a solipsistic sense) by the human mind and does not necessarily manifest the culmination of mental development or represent any absolute standard of truth, as he assumed. However, his assertion of the validity of psychic reality and of the existence of the unconscious was a major step in a different direction.

II

I return to the psychoanalytic situation. I spoke of the transference neurosis as a reenactment, a repetition by action. But a clinical psychoanalysis does not consist only of reenactments and their interpretations by the analyst. A considerable part of analysis is taken up not with dramatization but with narrative, not with dramatic play but with history. Narrative, historical account may be regarded as imitation of action, too, as a reproduction of action—not in the form of action, but in the form of memory in its more familiar mode as recollection. It is repetition of action, but here action is reproduced in mental representations (*Vorstellung*) and their symbolic expression in speech, not in reenacting the action. The action that is narrated may be a childhood experience or a current life experience (the latter, by the way, may be reenacted in the analytic session, too, instead of being recollected; as when a patient whose anger belongs to an event relating to her husband, vents this anger at the analyst, in the manner of a displacement). In recollection and its narration, the patient has a certain distance from the action, he has made the action an object of his contemplation, has objectified the action rather than being immersed in it. As I mentioned earlier, the dividing line between the two forms of remembering or repetition is not always sharply drawn: The patient who describes an experience with a great deal of affect is more identified

with that experience, is less objective about it; the past in-
vades the present. Such narration is closer to reenactment.

The repetition of action in the form of narrative may be
compared to a novel or to a historical account, the latter
perhaps the more dispassionate the account is. It is often
through the patient's detailed though fractionated accounts of
episodes of his history, remote or recent, that we get our first
knowledge of the development and character of his inner life.
The unfolding of the transference neurosis as reenactment
proceeds, in a more traditional analysis, by way of the analyst's interpreting interferences with the flow of reporting and
associating, and by interpreting certain directions or timings
in the drift of associations in terms of transference action.
The analyst gets indications of transference action from the
patient's nonverbal behavior, from certain sequences, and
from the timing and affective coloring of his narrative. The
injunction to free-associate rather than give a coherent narrative promotes the tension toward reenactment because everything that encourages the influence of unconscious currents,
including those generated by the actual presence of the analyst, is promoting reactivation rather than mere representational recollection of past experience.

One might be tempted to say that the patient's productions oscillate between transference dramatization and narrative (leaving reflection to one side for the moment), and there
is some truth to this. But we must keep in mind that language
itself is an essential element in human action once the child
has progressed to the verbal stage. That element of original
action, too, is repeated in drama. Language—speech—because of its central role in human action, is a dominant
element in drama, even though locomotion, pantomime, and
dance are also important elements in any performance. Language is not merely a means of reporting action, it is itself

action; narrative has a dramatic potential of its own. When not stultified by isolation from thought and fantasy, narrative tends to bring the original action to life again for the narrator and to conjure up the listener's similar or comparable memories, thoughts, and fantasies. Narrative and speech then move and act upon the narrator and the listener by their function as a symbolic expression of action.

In the course of the psychoanalytic process, narrative is drawn into the context of transference dramatization, into the force field of reenactment. Whether in the form of free association or of more consciously, logically controlled trains of thought, narrative in psychoanalysis is increasingly being revealed in its character as language action, as symbolic action, and in particular as language action within the transference force field. The emphasis, in regard to content and emotional tone of the communications through narrative, shifts more and more to their relevance as transference repetitions and transference actions in the psychoanalytic situation. One might express this by saying that we take the patient less and less as speaking merely *about* himself, about his experiences and memories, and more and more as symbolizing action in speech, as speaking from the depth of his memories, which regain life and poignancy by the impetus and urgency of reexperience in the present of the analytic situation.

All this does not ignore the fact that many of the patient's verbal communications in narrative form are important as historical data from which we can piece together his development and past experiences. They also serve as indications of what to expect about the development of the transference illness, and they give us information about the genetic and other aspects of the patient's symptoms, character traits, and specific reactions in the analytic situation. In the course of such narrative information, many new data, new memo-

ries, may come to light that modify and correct our understanding, give us important reorientations, and help us to
reorganize our material.

But none of this concerns psychoanalysis as an art and
the fantasy character of the analytic situation other than
indirectly. The art of psychoanalysis, with regard to the analyst, consists essentially in the handling of the transference.
The fantasy character of the psychoanalytic situation is its
character as play, in the double sense of children's and adults'
playing and of drama as a play. Play and fantasy have their
roots in life experience, draw their sustenance from it, and
give life its meaning. The dramatic play is a reenactment of life
in fantasy, and this fantasy life enters actual life, giving it
renewed and enriching meaning. The playing of the child, and
of the child in the adult, also has its roots in life experience
and gives meaning to life experience. The relative freedom
from constraints in play and fantasy life is not only a relief
from the exigencies of life, it also allows one to see beyond
those exigencies and not to be overwhelmed by their constraints in actual living.

For the small child, fantasy, play, and actual life experience are still one and the same reality. It is only later that
they become separated out as facets of a reality whose meaning is established in their interconnections. Thus the transference neurosis, on a regressive level of the patient's mental life,
is experienced by him as though he does not distinguish
between fantasy or memory and present actuality, whereas he
is capable, when functioning on more advanced mental levels,
of making this distinction and to profit from the revived
connections between them.

The art of the psychoanalyst, then, consists in a threefold
activity that is therapeutic: (1) He promotes that regression
that conjoins the patient's experiential past (memories and

fantasies) with his experiential present—the actuality of the analytic situation—so that they tend to become one. (2) The analyst, by appropriately timed and appropriately responsive interpretations and other interventions that speak to the reflective levels and capacities of the patient, reminds him of the difference between past and present, between memory-fantasy and actuality. (3) In doing so, the analyst helps the patient to reestablish connections, links between these different facets of reality, links that give renewed meaning to memories and fantasy life and to the patient's actual life in the present. Insofar as the patient's experiences in the analytic situation become part of his mental life, they influence his future life. All depends on the transference neurosis being recognized as the play of fantasy—a trial action in the sense in which Freud spoke of thought as trial and action—which shares in organizing reality, far from being unreal and therefore to be discarded. The resolution of the transference neurosis surely does not consist of renewed repression or any ultimate relinquishment of recovered memories and fantasies, but of employing them, revived and made available for development and change in the transference play, in actual living.

The developmental tasks of late adolescence in many respects are similar to those in an analysis. The so-called idealism of youth is often supposed to be given up in favor of the so-called realism of the adult. This realism of the disillusioned adult, in many quarters seen as the healthy norm or at least as all that we can aim for, is the result of the disruption, of the lack of live communication between youthful dreams and fantasies and what we call actual, rational life. Reality-testing is far more than an intellectual or cognitive function. It may be understood more comprehensively as the experiential testing of fantasy—its potential and suitability for actualization—and the testing of actuality—its potential for encompassing it in, and penetrating it with, one's fantasy life. We deal with the task of a reciprocal transposition.

I said that in the course of analysis narrative is drawn into the web of transference dramatization. In the more reflective phases, on the other hand, the patient's distance from himself and from the analyst gains ascendancy. What was reenactment, by reflection changes to that more objective repetition that Freud has called reproduction in the psychical field, as against reproduction by action. Reenactive memory then changes into that form of memory in which past and present objects and past and present self are clearly distinguished without losing each other. There are those phases in analysis when narrative and reflection are drawn into and yield to the force field of transference reenactment. And there are those other phases, not infrequently in the same hour, when reenactment is drawn into and yields to the force field of objectifying narrative and reflection. To hold to an optimal balance and to keep channels of communication open between these two is part of the analyst's art.

The celebrated good analytic hour—in my own experience as an analyst, rather an exception, but all the same a standard by which we measure our endeavors—shows something of the analyst's art. It shows even more that a piece of good analytic work is an artistic creation fashioned by patient and analyst in collaboration. For the most part such an hour does not come about by deliberate, premeditated steps or decisions on the analyst's part; it tends to proceed by virtue of the momentum of the process in which analyst and patient are engaged at a propitious time, although the soil from which such an hour grows is likely to have been prepared and cultivated by the analyst for a long time. The progression in such an hour is quite similar to the progression of a work of art, a poem, a musical composition, a painting, at a propitious

moment or period during the artist's work. There, too, it is
the momentum of an active imaginative process that creates
the next step, propelled by the directional tension of the
previous steps. This directional tension is the result of the
artist's imagination and the inherent force of his medium. A
word, a sound, a color, a shape—in the case of dramatic art an
action—or a sequence of these, once determined, strongly
suggests the next step to be taken. In the mutual interaction of
the good analytic hour, patient and analyst—each in his own
way and on his own mental level—become both artist and
medium for each other. For the analyst as artist his medium is
the patient in his psychic life; for the patient as artist the
analyst becomes his medium. But as living human media they
have their own creative capabilities, so that they are both
creators themselves. In this complex interaction, patient and
analyst—at least during some short but crucial periods—may
together create that imaginary life that can have a lasting
influence on the patient's subsequent actual life history.

In the movement toward reflection, the transference neurosis becomes apparent in its aspect as fantasy creation, which
has its own validity and function in the patient's life. While
intensely experienced, the transference feelings are prevented
from being acted upon, from materializing in deeds, so that
the transference neurosis seems to remain in the realm of trial
action. But insofar as the development, flowering, and resolution of the transference neurosis requires the active presence
of and responsive thought interaction with the analyst, and is
the result of the collaboration of patient and analyst, this
fantasy creation is more than an intrapsychic process—it has a
form of reality different from pure thought or dreaming or
daydreaming or remembering. The transference neurosis is
not only, as Freud called it, a transition between illness and
life; it is a transitional state between mere inner fantasy and

actuality. I am here in the neighborhood of Winnicott's "third area, that of play which expands into creative living and into the whole cultural life of man" (1967). Winnicott also speaks of patient and therapist playing together. As in the child's play, such fantasy action is called forth and shaped by present actuality (including the mental life of the analyst), and shapes present and future actuality. As a fantasy creation in which both patient and analyst in their different ways participate, the transference neurosis, as it is again and again contemplated and resolved in such reflection, has the potential for materially influencing the patient's conduct of his actual life.

I shall not discuss here the impact each transference neurosis, as lived through by the analyst with his patients, has on the analyst. This would require another full-length chapter. I also must forgo consideration of two issues that are closely related to my subject: the Aristotelian notion of catharsis or purgation through the arousal of pity and fear; and the function of the chorus in Greek tragedy, which in some respects resembles certain functions of the analyst. To the latter I have alluded earlier.

I shall close by trying to give another dimension to the dialectic of fantasy and actuality in pointing briefly to the child's and the parents' experience of the oedipal situation. The child experiences the oedipal strivings as powerful reality. In oversimplification, the little boy seriously wishes to marry his mother, the little girl her father. For the child prior to the passing of the Oedipus complex, these wishes are not just fleeting, unrealizable fantasies, but have the status of serious intentions and prospects. Understanding parents take these wishes seriously, too, but for them they are serious fantasies not to be acted on. They also may know, although often only intuitively, that these fantasy wishes are necessary ingredients of the child's psychosexual development, expressions of the child's beginning love life. In other words, the adult may understand that they are fantasies that are not in opposition to reality. While not to be realized in present actuality or with the actual parents at some future time, the oedipal strivings contribute to the formation of the full reality of life, as seen from the parental vantage point, from the viewpoint of the child's future. They are not fantasies to be given up or that, if not given up, must by necessity proliferate, unchanged, in the repressed unconscious, but fantasies that are indispensable factors in the full development of object relations and object love. The same, *mutatis mutandis*, is true for the fantasy character of the transference neurosis, as experienced by the child in the patient and as experienced by the analyst and by the patient as a reflecting adult.

Chapter Eight

Transcending the Limits of Revisionism and Classicism

GERALD I. FOGEL, M.D.

There seems to be something for everyone in Loewald, although that is part of the trouble in giving an account of him. "He is one of us," each of us proudly cries, preferring to disregard the fact that many self-proclaimed Loewaldians do not always agree among themselves on many important theoretical and clinical issues. Id, ego, and self psychologists, structural and object-relations theorists, adaptationalists, interactionalists, existentialists—all read Loewald and proclaim, "Now, *that* is what I have been trying to say all along!" Paradoxically, he is praised for his bold, pathfinding revision of classical theory, but also for his respect for and continued use of classical concepts.

I will argue that he is both revisionist and traditionalist, that he creates a theory that is at once new and old. I will also argue that the wide appeal of Loewald's ideas to so many varied psychoanalysts, and those ideas' apparent clinical relevance despite the absence of what we ordinarily call clinical data, cast light on the meaning, usefulness, and purpose of metapsychology.

His approach is interpretive, treating theoretical concepts as an analyst treats a patient's memories and ideas. Grounded in the here and now of the analytic situation, he seeks experiential reference points for every theoretical concept. Both new and old concepts are assumed to refer to real clinical phenomena, which, when more fully understood, may reveal hidden continuities as well as discontinuities and a heretofore unimaginable wider context. By observation, deconstruction, and imaginative reconstruction, Loewald helps us experience the subjective realities, past and present, to which the concepts refer. Theory may then come alive, to be reflected upon in all its complexity and ambiguity. Interpretation and continual reworking—a kind of theoretical working through—may then lead to new synthesis, integrity, and integration.

This boldly integrative approach to theoretical concepts is what Loewald calls the "authentic function" of psychoanalytic theory. He believes that "words, including concepts used in science, are living and enlivening entities in their authentic function" (1978a, p. 193). Psychoanalytic concepts can be redefined and reinterpreted, continually seen anew in the face of new data and ways of seeing, thus becoming transformed and transformative. Though he anticipated much of what is new in psychoanalysis in the past 30 years, he also anticipated a more recent integrative trend and a return to our roots—to classical theory and a close reading of Freud.

I will begin with a highly selective chronological account, follow with what I regard as Loewald's basic principles, then close by reemphasizing the power derived from the paradoxical affirmation of old and new in his work. I find it no straightforward matter to review or explain Loewald systematically, to do him full justice. A detailed summary of his work is impossible.

First, reading Loewald is slow going. He is evocative, poetic, but also dense, layered, ambiguous, and overdetermined.

An image, phrase, or paragraph may captivate, but the underlying complexity of his argument not be fully conveyed or
grasped. Quotations will elicit knowing responsiveness in
most readers, but where can one draw the line? No single
quotation can catch the full metaphorical richness or unique-
ness of his approach to a concept, which is circular, repetitive,
additive, and relies on the reader's integration of his many
different perspectives. His metaphors will ultimately frustrate
any who seek systematic closure, and he can seem vague,
amorphous. In most instances, however, these metaphors are
creative and integrative approaches to the inherent ambiguity
in the phenomena he examines. Retaining this essential ambiguity, he often reveals by allusion rather than by logical
deduction and exclusion. This partly accounts for the multiple appeal of his conceptions across theoretical divides. But
such a creative, poetic approach defies reduction or summary.
Repeated readings and a critical mass of clinical and theoretical experience are prerequisites for meaningful assimilation of
him.

Second, in the course of his work he ponders virtually
every important subject in psychoanalysis, and my selection
must leave out most of the particulars. Inevitably, it will be
insufficient for those who have not already read him in some
detail.

Finally, certain ideas and problems are *always* on his
mind. He refines these constantly, cannot ever be finished
with them, though they are often not explicit; they lie outside
or buried within the particulars of his immediate subject. I
shall return to this hidden content and the process of eternal
Loewaldian return further on. But all of these factors contribute to the difficulty of doing a straightforward review or easily
classifying him in relation to other theories or theorists.

A SELECTIVE CHRONOLOGICAL ACCOUNT

In his earliest analytic papers (1951, 1952, 1955), many of his major principles, basic assumptions, and new ideas are already present, although one cannot predict the astonishing unity and breadth of the paper on therapeutic action that was soon to follow.

Loewald stresses the central integrative and synthetic role of the ego, that its essence is "to maintain, on more and more complex levels of differentiation and objectivation, the original unity stemming from the primary narcissistic position" (1951, p. 16). The ego cannot be reduced to its defensive "function," or to any set of "functions." Both ego-id and reality-objects differentiate out of this original unity, and both, in health, are dynamic and continue to vitalize each other. Reality, in its essence, is neither objective, static, nor hostile. In neurosis, "reality" is not lost, but rather immature levels of the integration of ego and reality predominate over mature ones (1951).

He argues, as would others to follow, that the psychoanalytic theory of the time (primarily the ego psychology that was dominated by the work of Hartmann) had become too reductionistic, obsessive, and mechanistic—remote from clinical experience. Defense and conflict belong to the oedipal stage, he says, and many things must take place in analysis and in ego development that cannot be adequately conceptualized according to prevailing notions of conflict, defense, and defense analysis. Preoedipal stages—including preoedipal defenses, preoedipal objects (the mother, but also the preoedipal father), and immature ego states, where self-object differentiation cannot be taken for granted—must be addressed. The ubiquity and importance of varying levels of ego integration and of resumed development and new experience in the analysis of character and symptom are stressed. Problems of defense and of integration always coexist (1951, 1952).

His clinical nonreductionism is powerful and impressive. Except in detailed case presentations (which Loewald rarely uses), it is difficult to find a more convincing demonstration than in these early papers of the complexity of the actual patient, who contains all at once elements of mature ego, oedipal stage, defense, regression, fixation, immature ego states, primitive instinctual forces and magical thinking, creative adaptive solutions to unique developmental and cultural circumstances, and so forth. Even in this early schema, mature defenses may mask ego deficits, and ego deficits may obscure more mature ego capacities. But he never speaks (and never will) of "difficult" patients; he speaks rather of inadequate theory.

Unlike many theorists who would come later, he does not attack drive theory, but rather believes that ego psychology and clinical defense analysis have lost their necessary rootedness in instinctual life and its liberation. This liberation of instinctual forces is important in its own right and in many instances occurs for the first time in analysis, as a new version of something old (1955, p. 41). He argues that this knowledge, and the necessary rootedness of psychoanalysis in the primal and the infantile, have become lost in the cerebral and overly mechanized conceptions of current theory. Ego psychology has forgotten something that id psychology knew: Drives and reality, drives and objects cannot exist in isolation from each other.

The paper on therapeutic action (1960) continues to astonish because of its scope and unity and how far ahead of its time it still seems to be. Presented in 1957 it was not published until 1960. One can find almost everything in

Loewald in this paper. Over the next 30 years he would widen his field of observation, and refine and elaborate his basic ideas and principles. But this is the nuclear paper that crystallized and unified his thought, and predicted most of the lines of thought he would later pursue.

His psychoanalytic, psychiatric, intellectual, and personal forebears are not present in or inferable from the text or references, which are mostly to Freud and a few classic contributions on transference. Most of the object relations, interpersonal, self psychology, or developmental people were not widely known to American psychoanalysts. Melanie Klein was largely unassigned and unread in this country at that time. Loewald refers to her once in an earlier paper, but one cannot see her influence in his work. Fairbairn's and Winnicott's early papers had begun to appear, as had some early papers by Jacobson and Mahler, but he seems to anticipate the centrality of these conceptions, and certainly the integrative efforts within the analytic mainstream that came much later. Kernberg and Kohut were not yet in print.

Undoubtedly, Loewald derived some of his developmental sensibilities from his child therapy training and his interpersonal sensibilities from his exposure to Sullivan and Fromm-Reichmann during the years of his analytic training in Baltimore in the '40s, shortly after he came to the United States from Europe. Despite their clinical and therapeutic richness, however, these interpersonal schools virtually exclude any intrapsychic emphasis, and perhaps this accounts for the lack of their tangible presence in Loewald's writings and possible lack of usefulness to him in his theory-building.

Cooper (1988) has given us a detailed, elegant review of this breakthrough paper. I can mention only some of the important core concepts that were introduced in it. First, the analyst as a new object; this is the first so-called classical paper to place interaction with the analyst and resumption of ego development at the center of the therapeutic process. Second, the emerging core; the analyst reflects "aspects of undistorted reality" in countless ways (mainly by interpretation), structuring and channeling the patient's own experience, recognizable as such. Here is an "empathy" concept most analysts can live with. Third, a new conception of analytic neutrality, a passionately argued challenge of the notion of the completely "objective" analyst. Fourth, the id as an organization related to reality and objects; drives are inherently related to and organized within object relations; drives organize reality and vice versa; the new object found in analysis is also an instinctual, infantile object.

Fifth, significant analogies between therapeutic process (interpretation) and mother–infant interaction (handling); again, this is in a form most analysts can live with, one that does not seem to smack of infantilization, inappropriate gratification, or naive reconstructions to infancy. Sixth, the metaphor of a higher organization (the analyst) in interaction with a lower organization (the patient) in the therapeutic process, with a "tension" between, across which the patient "reaches." Here is a "tilt" most analysts can live with, untainted somehow by patronization or paternalism, suggestion or indoctrination. Seventh, the notion of disorganization and reorganization in analysis, leading to integration on a higher level, with two sides to interpretation: into the original depth via regression and deconstruction, and into a higher level by interpretation and reconstruction. Eighth, the importance of love and truth, expressed through and subordinate to a love of truth in the analytic relationship. Ninth, transference as the intrapsychic corollary of the interpersonal, which recaptures the lost depths, making it possible to change ghosts (unconscious complexes) to ancestors (well-integrated psychic structure) via a transitional demon (regressive transference) stage. Tenth, transference as crucial to health, not mere pathology. Finally, the "integrative experience longed for," a newly formulated inherent developmental and clinical tendency toward higher integration.

In the early '70s (1971a, 1973) this developmental tendency is further expanded and reconceptualized theoretically and clinically and placed at the center of Loewald's theory. Organizing activity defines the "basic way of functioning of the psyche." Internalization, the generating of symbolic representations and other aspects of instinctual activity, individuation, clinical interpretation, language—all these and more, including many classical concepts, are reformulated as varieties of this inherent tendency toward disorganization and reorganization on a higher level.

Many drive-psychological terms are reconceptualized as organizing activities: cathexis, narcissistic cathexis, hypercathexis, mnemic image, experience of satisfaction, the linking of the unconscious "thing presentation" with the preconscious "word presentation," and so forth. All refer to real clinical and developmental events that make drive, object, thought, action, and mind indivisible. Clinical interpretation of deeply regressive but analytically structured transference is the unique analytic action that facilitates this organizing activity. The fundamental analytic assumption is that all mental activity is personally motivated (1971a, p. 103).

In other papers, additional dimensions of instinct theory are elaborated: instincts and language, the nature of primary process, and the rootedness of all of psychic life in the body and in so-called primitive wishes and needs. Language facilitates higher organization and differentiation, but also retains magical-evocative powers to link with and regain the "original density" of the primary process, thereby allowing the recovery of psychic health in its full vitality and original unity (1978a).

I can refer only briefly to his important papers on clinical process: the transference neurosis (1971b), the analytic process (1970), and the analytic situation (1975), which utterly defy summary. He does not shrink from the many ambiguities and difficulties in integrating theoretical concepts into actual clinical work, especially the peculiar but characteristically analytic blend of subjective and objective, of personal and interpersonal, contained in the phenomena of the transference neurosis.

The transference neurosis is an ideal construct, a complex creation that links present actuality potential with past actuality potential. It is living, not static; changing and changeable. It is an intrapsychic experience ("in" the mind) that occurs in a special and necessary relational (both interactional and intersubjective) context. It is an "imitation of action in the form of action," a reenactment on the stage of internality. However, the original "action" is a conglomerate of oedipal, preoedipal, and adolescent experience that is reorganized and reinterpreted according to the analyst's and patient's present modes of understanding (1975, p. 358). Thus it is new experience, but also a new version of something very old, a "preservation" in the mind. In its ambiguous qualities, and with its emphasis on creativity and play, this experience has much in common with Winnicott's transitional experience, which is "intermediate"—it partakes of both internal and external reality but is never entirely reducible to the terms of one or the other. Loewald himself notes this.

Thus the reality-generating nature of the interpretive act is stressed, as well as the marriage of creative imagination and so-called facts in analytic truth. Deterministic and aesthetic approaches to knowledge are but different facets of unified mental activity.

Finally, in several recent papers on the oedipus complex and the self (1979, 1985), he closes a circle. He began his work by rejecting a too-narrow focus on defense analysis, on oedipal-level work, as reductionistic and constrictive. His attention turned to immature ego states, intersubjective and interpersonal aspects of analysis, and the altered understandings and interpretive activities that were required of the analyst. Now, after a lifetime of discovery and thought, he reaffirms the centrality of the oedipal stage for all analytic work.

He does this by redefining the oedipal stage with an emphasis on the emergence of the capacity for self-reflection, personal responsibility, and individuality—the capacity to be an individual; object, object relations, and self, in the analytic intrapsychic sense, do not exist until the oedipal stage. Thus, as I read him, the analyst's link to the "emerging core" is not a vaguely loving empathic link but a recognition of the patient's capacity for being, and necessity to be, "separate," to create and be responsible for a unique symbolic-representational personal experience, necessarily suffer guilt and atonement, and therefore become able to join "the moral order of the race." Individuation, oedipal conflict and resolution, the emerging core, and the search and responsibility for personal meaning become conjoined, linked. The oedipal stage is restored to its place at the center of all (individual) human development and clinical analytic work.

Further, through a sophisticated discussion of parricide and incest, he brings the narcissistic and the preoedipal directly into the oedipal core. There are resonances with Melanie Klein's depressive position in the stress on guilt and reparation, and with Kohut and Winnicott in the symbiotic and transitional character of oedipal experience as Loewald defines it here (1979).

I believe that the "classical" neurotic patient becomes irrelevant, no longer exists in Loewald's paradigm. The analyst may recognize nascent capacities for self-reflection and personal responsibility and cocreate an oedipal-level analysand. Although a variable preoedipal core that varies in its accessibility to analysis *may* be more common in our time, many "difficult" patients may appear less so as these former difficulties with theory become clarified.

THE BASIC LOEWALDIAN PRINCIPLES

I see an overriding, centrally important first principle in Loewald, something that is his most basic assumption. It is not any sort of entity in the usual sense, because it assumes no structure of its own, nor is it force or energy as we ordinarily conceive these terms. But it makes things "go." It goes by many names in his work but is most clearly articulated when he speaks of internalization. Here is a pure, succinct statement: "Internalization . . . is conceived as the basic way of functioning of the psyche, not as one of its functions" (1973, p. 71).

Internalization is the organizing activity that is the very essence of, that defines and constructs, the human mind. It is at once path, goal, and product—a growth principle, an inherent developmental tendency. At the level of personal experience it is a wish, a longing. In the paper on therapeutic action (1960), before Loewald has fully defined and made central this first principle, he refers to its appearance clinically and developmentally as the "integrative experience longed for," and its discernible and articulatable structured representations are the "emerging core," the potential to which the analyst or parent must attend and respond.

Because he conceives of internalization broadly and derives it from nothing more "elemental," nothing that precedes or "causes" it, and nothing that can be separated from its own dynamic actuality, so to speak, it is difficult to compare his usage to that of others. I think he uses the term in a way no one else does. Although he speaks of degrees of internalization, he does not dwell on fine distinctions between different types of internalization. He does not go into systematic detail regarding what is internalized when, except to say it involves complex interactional processes, nor does he give convincing examples to illustrate particular internalizations.

Like psychic energy for Freud, internalization is a given for Loewald, revealed only by its manifestations, never able to be directly grasped or simply defined. Unlike Freud's concept, this "force" is given no more tangible metaphorical qualities. It has no quantity to be measured or weighed. It refers to pure process. It is *represented* by the *concept* of the coherent ego. Loewald's coherent ego is characterized by the internalization process yet is also the product of that same process. Internalization, for Loewald, reflects cohesive structure formation, and cohesive structure is different from and mutually exclusive of continued unconscious fantasy relations with objects. Although internalization is reversible (1973, pp. 339–340), the term refers to an expansion of the "ego core," reflecting integration and mastery.

Trends opposing internalization are also broadly conceived and accepted as inevitable. Repression-defense is that which splits off parts of the mind and makes them inaccessible for assimilation and integration. Identification may blur self-object discriminations beyond their developmentally appropriate time, creating false unity. These constrict the coherent ego, compromise and blind it, and are growth- and truth-limiting.

Internalization is not an inside-outside thing. "It" seeks unity without sacrificing discrimination. Useful access to preoedipal instinctual and cognitive modes is preserved. The older psychoanalytic term with which it has most in common is probably *structuralization*, but the underlying assumptions and values of many who use that term are not the same as Loewald's underlying assumptions and values. For example, internalization is not an abstract, value-free process, but correlates with healthy development, adaptation, accommodation, assimilation, differentiation, integration, creativity, and clarity. It is not the synthetic function of traditional structural theory, whose creativity serves neurosis as well as truth.

A second Loewaldian principle: The mind contains no static entities, no reified structures. Psychic reality is always dynamic, always process; when Loewald is being more precise, he speaks of process-structures. Everything is related to everything else in the mind. Living systems within larger systems are whole systems in their own right, yet interrelate and interconnect with each other in countless necessary and ever more all-encompassing and intricate ways. Although our field of observation is limited to the human mind, there is no way to define a precise limit or border to this mind.

Friedman (1990) astutely notes that Loewald sees structures as processes that point in certain directions; wishes and thoughts, motives and representations are not fated to be in different frames of reference. Each may evolve into more highly structured, more meaningful patterns. The whole mind moves (or can move) in the direction of *higher* organization. At the level of theory, Loewald cannot abide talk of ego "functions," or of ego and reality as if they were distinct and separated worlds. The *mind* makes distinctions and also has the potential to integrate, even transcend these distinctions in higher organizations. Words and concepts are the basic Loewaldian entities—changing and changeable, yet our only lights in this wilderness of flux and impermanence. Language is therefore given a central place in Loewald.

A third Loewaldian principle: Although everything that can be apprehended—drives, structures, objects—is created in and by the mind, and nothing exists from the start separate from the mind that can conceive it, this developmental, organizing activity cannot be done alone. It rather takes place in a context, within a "force field" *codetermined*, fatefully, by human objects. This codetermining process can be created in all its power in the analytic situation. By shifting focus from drive to mind as organizing activity, Loewald fools some into thinking he is an object relations theorist, because mind contains and creates self and other; therefore, there is always an "*other*" coexisting with ego/self and with motive/desires. Additionally, it is impossible to develop a perceiving, meaning-generating mind, or to achieve the necessary degree of internalization to become and to be able to be sustained as an individual outside a personal network of necessary human relations.

But there is a crucial paradox here. Human life and human development are inseparably embedded in a matrix of object relations. But full humanness requires the acceptance of separateness—essential aloneness as the price of reflective self-awareness; individuation, the achieving of internalized object relations, coincides with the inescapable necessity of accepting personal responsibility for one's own fate in the face of it. The frame of reference of clinical psychoanalysis— Loewald's frame—is intrapsychic experience, the study of the "individual psyche" (1973, p. 70), the single, unique, mean-ing-generating mind.

A fourth Loewaldian principle: isomorphism. Systems or structures that have similar or identical structure or form are defined as isomorphic. It is essential to recognize that the presence of isomorphic structures does not imply that one is necessarily derived from or superordinate to or explanatory of the other. Friedman (1990) was the first to note this isomorphism, which I find to be absolutely consistent at all levels of abstraction in Loewald. Loewaldian isomorphism is a crucially important aspect of his theory and accounts for a good deal of the cohesiveness and consistency in it, as you will soon see. From sometimes differing and sometimes over-lapping vantage points, the therapeutic relationship, the ther-apeutic process, insight and change, the normal mind, human development, and human individuation all reflect the same process-structure: the evolutionary, developmental tendency toward disorganization and reorganization at higher levels. These are all isomorphs for internalization.

About instinctual activity: ". . . the basic postulate con-cerning the general function of the psychic apparatus is . . . that of generating mental representatives of these [organis-mic] stimuli, that is, generating instinctual activity. And my accent is not on the fact that instincts are mental representa-tives of organismic stimuli, but on the fact that they are mental representatives" (1971a, p. 119). Instincts are givens, but even more important, they also organize and are organized by mind. On another level, interpretation and insight are isomorphs. Of interpretation: ". . . we have no other way of applying our mind, whether in observation and understand-ing or in action. It is only in a context of meanings, when interpretations have become commonplace, that we speak of the material in questions as 'facts'" (1971a, p. 102). "Facts" are givens, but even more important, they also organize and are organized by mind.

The basic way of functioning of the mind is internalization, is to generate representations as the central aspect of its instinctual activities, is to interpret—to construct facts and meanings, is to differentiate and integrate self and other on the path to individuation, and so on. These are all organizing, "linking" activities. At the clinical level, the ever more complexly differentiated parts are integrated and synthesized in a higher meaning that combines past and present, fantasy and reality, memory and perception, self and other.

A fifth and final principle: psychic reality, as Loewald construes it, has inherent values, is not morally neutral. This goes beyond superego morality. It is rather an extension of the potential inherent tendencies for self-reflection, personal responsibility, and integration. I have already noted that internalization is not a value-free concept.

Further, the analyst optimally reveals these values in his best analytic work. In his tribute to Loewald, Schafer (1990) takes up aspects of Loewald's conception of the analyst as new object for the patient and goes directly to the clinical heart of this matter. He speaks of analytic love and of Loewald's approaching the matter through his conceptions of "holding in trust the ego core or potential self of the analysand through all the trials of analysis, and also when he speaks of the analyst seeing the patient as more than he or she can yet conceive and thereby taking on the responsibility of safeguarding a future for that person" (Schafer 1990).

Schafer rarely lacks his own words for what he wants to say, but in this instance he uses a description by Rilke of Cézanne's relationship to what he painted and a lengthy and beautiful quotation from Loewald's work in which scientific detachment, objective analyzing, and object love—compassion for the whole patient's being—are said to flow from the same source (1970, p. 297). My understanding of this is that at its core, the analyst's best efforts to understand the patient, the reverence for truth, and the efforts to reach for its inexhaustible and rarely attainable completeness are synonymous with love and represent the analyst's way of seeking the "integrative experience longed for."

To my mind, there is nothing sentimentalizing or simplifying about this attitude as I find it in Loewald. It is idealistic in its insistence on the realizable human potential for full integration, personal responsibility, unity, and transcendence. But it does not sacrifice rationality or hard truths to loving kindness. Its goals are integrative states, not oceanic ones.

HIDDEN PERSPECTIVES—NEW AND OLD

The attempt to find continuity and integration in the paradoxical amalgam of old and new and in the interplay and tension between them is one of the hidden tasks Loewald works on endlessly. Understanding the ambiguous relationship between the personal and the interpersonal in human experience is another. I turn now to two additional perspectives—one new and one old—that I also find always present, but rarely spelled out in his work.

The first perspective that is all-pervasive, yet hidden in Loewald's theory and revision of existing theory, is his *worldview*. Although only rarely referred to explicitly (e.g., 1971a, pp. 110–111), it may be inferred, I believe, from all of his psychoanalytic writings. It is entirely new relative to the worldview that was the context in which many traditional psychoanalytic concepts developed, and refers to Loewald's basic assumptions and deepest convictions about the nature of reality—what I shall call *superordinate* or *absolute* reality, to distinguish it from *psychic* reality. Schafer (1990) points out that, for Loewald, this is not the received reality of Western civilization, of positivistic philosophy, or of natural science. In this newer view, reality is conceived of as pure process. In this non-Newtonian, non-Cartesian, nonlinear, nondualistic universe there are no solid entities, no static concepts or structures, no first causes. Elementary particles cannot be isolated for inspection, but rather create energy fields and momentum that interact with neighboring particles and their fields.

Reality consists of complex hierarchal *dynamic* systems or structures in complex relations to each other. No part can simply or reductionistically be derived from another part. Nothing is constant or permanent; there is continual movement, change, and flow. From the standpoint of human awareness, there is no mind-body split, no simple "objective" or "external" reality; observer and observed inevitably influence and alter each other.

Additionally, there is an underlying unity in this conception. Whole systems are organismic. All parts exist and are defined in relation to all other parts and in their entirety comprise a single living system—whether a mind, a biological entity, an ecological system, a solar system, or the universe itself is referred to.

I can easily imagine that Loewald conceives of a universe that functions on a basic principle of eternal disorganization and reorganization, decomposition and recomposition, evolution and decay—perhaps bearing some kinship to the eternal cycles of creation and destruction, birth and death, of Buddhist philosophy, Nietzsche's conception of eternal return, or Freud's Eros and Thanatos as broad cosmic principles.

These ideas are compatible with now deeply established trends in contemporary science, philosophy, linguistics, and the arts—physical indeterminacy and relativity in physics, existential philosophy, structuralism, hermeneutics, systems theory. These ideas have been in the air in the twentieth century and are sometimes referred to as an "emerging" paradigm. Loewald's thought continually reflects these sensibilities. It is probably relevant that he refers to philosophy as his first love and that he studied philosophy with Martin Heidegger before studying medicine (1980, p. viii).

In his analytic writings, Loewald confines himself to the study of the nature of the mind, especially as revealed through the psychoanalytic process and situation. He speaks therefore only of psychic reality. But I believe that his worldview, his deepest belief in the nature of things, leads him to suppose that the mind works according to the same general principles and laws that superordinate or absolute reality does. *These realities—psychic reality and absolute reality—are isomorphic: they share the same underlying structure, though one is not to be regarded as being superordinate to, causally related to, explanatory of, or derived from the other.*

Loewald's worldview is reflected in the aesthetic and spiritual qualities in his work, his embrace of the nonrational and the eternal, his emphasis on "preservation" in the field of the mind, and his stress on the crucial synthetic and potentially transcendent roles of art and creative imagination; it casts light on his stress on unity as the beginning and possible achievable end of human development.

Paradoxically, he respects determinism and science, and identifies strongly with Freud and with being a physician. He seems disciplined, patient, realistic, practical. He finds fault with Jung's psychology, for example, for its predisposition to take refuge in the "mystical" and other "higher" realms. He does not dilute the Freudian universals: the reality principle, instinctual life, conflict. These can be integrated without escapism, he says, via ego expansion and sublimation—a genuine transcendence (1977, p. 416). The truth he seeks, however, the mind he wishes to understand, embraces the philosophic, the aesthetic, and the spiritual, as well as an expanded view of science. This is not a simple theory.

His conception of reality affects everything he thinks about—every topic. He does not think in neat, systematic, linear modes, nor does he conceive that anything important that happens in human beings takes place in such modes. Human beings live, develop, maintain, and sustain themselves in cycles of eternal return. This is not "theory" for Loewald in the abstract sense, or a consciously chosen "philosophy of life" in the superficial sense. It is the nature of human life as he sees it. It is in his bones, so to speak.

The second perspective that is all-pervasive yet hidden in Loewald's theory and revision of existing theory is his clinical stance, his analytic methodology and technique. This unbroken tradition of psychoanalytic practice is old; despite major advances in technique, certain of its essential features extend in an unmodified line back to Freud. Two observations about Loewald allow me to infer that he belongs to this unbroken tradition.

First, despite the obvious fact of the groundbreaking nature of his work over more than 30 years of ferment and change in psychoanalysis, the enlarging of our vision of what analysis is and what we may analyze, there is nothing in that work that encourages a reader to alter standard analytic technique. I refer not to the notable absence of clinical data or discussions of technique from his work, but to attitudes and emphases that pervade his writing and continually remind us that this is a classical analyst who treats patients in traditional ways: the emphasis on understanding, on putting things into words, on the centrality of transference, interpretation, and insight; the gentle insistence that the patient bear reality and assume responsibility for his or her own experience; the reluctant respect for the limitations on what we can know and what or who may be analyzable; the belief that analytic principles and analytic truth cannot be derived from realms outside the analytic situation itself, including the patient's so-called real early life; even the tolerance for ambiguity and mystery at the borders of clinical and theoretical understanding, the loose ends as well as the wonder and humility that go with constant work on the edge of "the depths." Despite his appreciation of the interpersonal and intersubjective aspects of analysis, I do not easily imagine him trying to *alter technique*—for example, to increase his empathy or the analytic "hold," or to confront his analysands sooner with their projective identifications. His tone, demeanor, and modes of conceptualization convey to me a clinical stance that I associate with traditional methodology and technique.

Second, despite the astonishing fact that it contains almost no clinical data, Loewald's work is nevertheless almost entirely clinical. We recognize this intuitively. The work does not seem "metapsychological," at least as that word is often used—for theory that is abstracted away from experience. It is theory, but it is not "experience-distant." It is a way of conceptualizing experience that remains recognizable as such. His theory *feels* rooted in clinical analytic experience, despite the absence of particular detailed examples.

These two factors—traditional methodology and technique and the traditional rooting of theory in the actual experience of doing and being in analysis—are crucial factors that help Loewald establish continuity with our psychoanalytic past. He assumes that important experiential commonalities exist in the psychoanalytic process of today and yesterday, despite changes in the way that process is conceptualized. He is therefore free to reexamine concepts that others reject out of hand because of their abstract theoretical connotations in the context of modern thinking. His reformulations always seek the experiential roots of concepts. When his theoretical constructions and reconstructions are successful, they facilitate theoretical integration—a new creation, as he puts it, at a higher level of organization.

To summarize, I think that a very important new thing in Loewald is his worldview, his conception of the basic nature of reality. Much of his theoretical work can be viewed as an effort to integrate these radically new assumptions within a historical perspective that seeks and recognizes common experiential bonds across cultural, temporal, and theoretical boundaries, within the potentially cohesive and unifying tradition defined by analytic practice beginning with Freud. Although virtually every subject he considers is altered by the ambiguous and paradoxical nature of the new reality (and new clinical realities) he ponders, he has to throw out little of what he values in the old completely; instead, he throws them in a new light through theoretical-experiential reconstruction.

The wish and need in Loewald not to do violence to either of these hidden perspectives—new worldview and traditional technique—contribute importantly to his extraordinary capacity to build integrative bridges between current and classical ways of understanding ourselves and our world. This is why Loewald's theorizing, like good Loewaldian clinical interpretations, embraces old and new and restructures them in a higher integration—a new creation, as he puts it, at a higher level of organization.

THE CENTRAL LOEWALDIAN PARADOX

I have now delineated principles and perspectives that I believe organize Loewald's work as a whole, that give it its overall structure. I hope that doing so has conveyed how unified and cohesive that body of work is, as well as the sources for some of its power. But I will not be surprised if it has had a monochromatic quality for some readers, especially those who are not already close readers and appreciators of his work. It is as if I had described the structure of the symphonic form without letting the hearer listen to any particular symphonies. As one must listen to music, so one will be convinced, or not, of this structure and its organizing power only by absorbing the many clinical, theoretical, and cultural phenomena Loewald has illuminated by it in his work, and by the evocativeness of his individual examples. But readers must read these for themselves. It is impossible to convey these particulars within the confines of a single chapter.

But I must reiterate what I see as the central Loewaldian paradox. Which of these two statements is true? Statement one: Loewald's theory is a radical revision of basic Freudian theory; he is a revolutionary in disguise, too far from tradition to pretend to be a traditionalist. Statement two: Loewald's theory preserves almost every important traditional emphasis. I submit that both are true.

He is revolutionary in that he rejects Freudian theoretical bedrock. He rejects biology as a basis from which to *derive* psychology (although the biological and bodily basis of human experience remains centrally important). Psychoanalysis is a humanity, or perhaps a discipline which respects the principles and values of humanistic traditions as well as natural science ones. He rejects dualism and a positivist view of reality—the so-called objective reality of natural science.

He rejects the primacy of drives as conceived in classic theory. Drives are psychological, representational—products of differentiation and differentiating elements in an experiential, interpersonal, and intersubjective field. He rejects the view that there is an inherent antagonism between drives (ego, organism) and environment (parents, civilization). Drives, ego, and objects are created by the mind out of original unity in a context of human relationships. Full internalization, full integration is a potentially realizable ideal—the recovery of original unity as a goal of healthy development.

He is revolutionary in that he radically redefines almost every important concept he examines. His nondualistic view of reality contributes significantly. An example is how his definitions of ego and internalization and of drive and object cocreate each other. Unlike traditional structural conceptions, these definitions carry no characteristics that can be simply represented by a spatial entity; "structure" and "process" are not clearly separable; both are defined by the inherent tendency toward organization.

Similarly, Loewald's superego and id cannot be usefully conceived of without clinical reference points or a full grasp of their relationships within a field in process. The "components" of internalization are not "subtypes" visualizable as varying types and degrees of something "outside" becoming "inside," but rather are degrees of differentiation and integration of a living developmental, interactional, and, most important, intrapsychic process.

His conceptions of the oedipal stage and transference neurosis are totally unlike classic conceptions, partly because they are not bound to a linear or dualistic conception of time. They are defined by the human capacity to reflect upon personal experience and to assume responsibility for it. History exists as an aspect of the human potential to realize it and appropriate it. Childhood is not unimportant—quite the contrary. But "objective" time is not relevant here. For all his immersion in what we call the narcissistic or preoedipal, one never catches Loewald speculating on what comes "first" in the live patient.

Thus, though he sees development as necessarily occurring over time, he has integration–interruption events occurring in the oedipal "stage," oedipal-level structural events occurring in adolescence, "preoedipal" patients having crucially important oedipal characteristics according to how they behave in analysis, "primitive" components in normal neurosis and health. He blurs these categories so thoroughly that one questions their usefulness as categories. In fact, he himself rarely uses them. Ambiguity and paradox are thereby introduced into almost every traditional category. All phenomena are defined according to their context—their structural and process *relationships* to every other discernible aspect in the situation. There are few useful one-liner definitions of an important clinical–theoretical concept in Loewald.

But Loewald also preserves almost every traditional emphasis. He is traditional in rigorously confining his data-collecting and speculation to the clinical analytic situation and process. He is traditional in his deep belief in the centrality of the infantile origins of adult character and their full emergence in a deep, regressive transference neurosis, and in the central role of verbalization, interpretation, and insight in its resolution. He is traditional in his belief that all that is good and bad in human beings derives from these same infantile roots, and in his ultimate emphasis on the intrapsychic.

He is traditional in his belief in the primacy of the oedipal stage, superego development, and (to a lesser extent) castration anxiety. That he redefines these to incorporate aspects of development and adult experience conceptualized by others as nonoedipal only serves to emphasize his classic position.

Though "objective" truth is no longer to be had, though truth is now conceived as a created process, truth, love of truth, and the personal nature of truth also remain central. Love, grace, action, fate in the form of one's early environment—these are real and crucial, necessary to acknowledge, and important components of what analysts do and deal with. But these factors are not sufficient, nor are they superordinate in defining analysis and analytic work. Insight remains central—finding out the truth.

He retains the central importance of instincts or drives, especially for clinical work. In fact, he rescues and reaffirms certain values and emphases from id psychology. Liberation of instinctual forces is crucial. Instinct is now representational, but remains "the most primitive element or unit of motivation" (1971a, p. 119). Instincts as the life of the body remain central—life as it is lived, nothing "higher." Instinct plays a powerful role in his conception of original unity. The primary process is vital to the flow and continuity of life in linking present to past, to the "lifelong creativity of the personal past," as well as to the "preservation" that is an essential part of the mind's linking activity. Language has an essential primary process aspect in its core, vital sense. It is magical-evocative, not just in the sense of stirring feeling, but also in its power to establish contact with the depths of mental life.

He is also traditional in his retention of views and values inherent in ego psychology. He is a "structuralist" whose spirit has much in common with Rapaport and Hartmann. Complex hierarchical organizations, the centrality of concepts of integration and differentiation, multiple function (though he rarely uses the term), and organization are the watchwords. The guiding values of ego psychology are Loewald's values: multiple points of view and a nonreductionistic, nonjudgmental clinical stance.

Loewald does not like the breaking of things into cognitive parts that seem, unlike the mind he knows, separable from each other, but he sees the psychic agencies as meaningful organizing concepts, and the idea of increasingly complex organizations is structural in the ego-psychological sense. I have already noted that Loewald's internalization concept has much in common with ego psychology's structuralization concept. He insists, however, that living structure as process or process-structure is always dynamic. But he is structural. Internalization and structuralization proceed, in one of their most important aspects, from identificatory processes that occur in connection with highly complex interactional processes.

I have stated earlier how Loewald accomplishes this neat trick of being both revolutionary and classicist—by the most *analytic* of methods. He *assumes* that important continuities and commonalities exist between our clinical-experiential-theoretical past and present, and he discerns and integrates these by deconstruction, imaginative reconstruction, and interpretation. He tests the metaphors and concepts of the intellectual and scientific climate of his time and of psychoanalytic tradition against clinical reality as he can apprehend it directly. Safely rooted to the experiential realities of clinical process, he does not have to throw out concepts merely because they connote outmoded conceptions of so-called objective reality. He is interested in their clinical-experiential meanings.

An example that will be familiar to most readers is in the paper on therapeutic action (1960). This paper was astonishingly ahead of its time, a revolutionary break with traditional models. Yet, paradoxically and intriguingly, in the final section of this early paper he argues passionately for the recovery of the "original richness of interrelated phenomena and mental mechanisms" that the concept of transference encompassed. Here is the famous metaphor where the transference neurosis is said to be "due to the blood of recognition, which the patient's unconscious is given to taste so that the old ghosts may reawaken to life," and where he goes on to equate the work of analysis with the laying to rest of these revitalized ghosts so that they might be transformed into "ancestors" (1960, pp. 246–249).

The metaphor, he reminds us, is borrowed directly from Chapter 7 of Freud's dream book, and he quotes from several other pre-1900 Freudian texts. Loewald uses Freud's language of energy flow, libido, and cathexis easily and unself-consciously here, as he persuades us of the clinical phenomena to which they refer: the vital, powerful, and timeless unconscious complexes that, when released in analysis, enrich and revitalize psychic life—object and self, ego and reality—as they do in normal development. He reminds us that what was once called catharsis and later conceptualized as the "automatic unwinding of the libido" (Ferenczi and Rank 1924) signified necessary *intrapsychic* analytic events. By resurrecting Freud's almost passing reference to the additional meaning of transference as the flow from unconscious to preconscious, he reminds us of the advantage of Freud's metaphor in forcing us to remember that we are referring to intrapsychic events when we speak analytically of transference and that Freud "knew" this in some sense, although he did not yet have the language of the representational world that would later make it more precisely articulatable. As an unconscious wish through a dream fastens onto a day residue, so an unconscious object cathexis (what we now call a persisting infantile wish attached to its infantile object, an unconscious fantasy relationship) may fasten onto the available preconscious (intrapsychic) object, the analyst.

The transference neurosis remains his central process concept. Loewald does not replace it with his new emphasis on object relations and intersubjective phenomena. Far from abandoning it, he gives it new life, as an intrapsychic event that takes place inevitably—developmentally and analytically—in an interpersonal and intersubjective field. The term is transformed and enriched by the new and the old. His metaphor resonates in both the intrapsychic and the interpersonal realms, while his theoretical range helps us separate these realms where it is important and possible to do so. A concept that in 1960 was looking ghostlike tasted the fresh blood of Loewaldian object-relations theory and reestablished its links to some very pale conceptual ghosts that had haunted our theory, disturbed our rest.

Loewald is interested in the clinical or developmental events signaled by these terms; he can examine them in this light without fear of taint by their metaphorical connections to concrete, physicalistic quantities of energy flow or linear conceptions of time. We can, in this example, reread Freud and see the continuity between our experience and his, and turn theoretical ghosts—the terms cathexis, libidinal flow, Pcs., transference neurosis—into honored ancestors. Freud's terms are disassembled, the clinical and developmental (interpersonal, intersubjective, and intrapsychic) events signified are reconstructed, then reorganized more meaningfully according to Loewald's own metaphors.

In addition, we may then use these terms or lay them to rest with equanimity, according to our own beliefs, temperament, or needs; should we discard them, we will have a greater chance to understand when we read or when others use them. We can judge whether the term is used to conceptualize real clinical events or not, rather than prejudging any who use the term as know-nothings who prefer schools and theories that are not our own.

Loewald shares, I think, Sandler's (1983) attitude toward traditional theory. Sandler speaks of the elasticity of psychoanalytic concepts, or the need to try to understand the context in which the term was used and for what purposes; one should not assume that because a term means different things in different contexts that it has no use, or insist rigidly that it can only mean the thing *we* say it means. The more "elastic" or flexible attitude is a useful guard against the needless constraints and unneccessary reification that comes from defining psychoanalytic terms *too* systematically.

To reiterate, I believe that Loewald is at once both radical revisionist and classicist. He safeguards our emerging analytic core *and* preserves our necessary genetic theoretical antecedents. He performs each of these roles so elegantly that on that basis alone one might suspect that he is more than both, that he transcends the limits that such terms may suggest. He resists classification fiercely. I have suggested that he transcends these categories in some higher organization—an integration of old and new, clinical-theoretical past and present.

He is, however, in the strongest Freudian tradition of not being able to turn his back on anything that seems to him to be true. If he cannot make sense of it *yet*, he keeps looking and trying to understand. Staying true to apparently divergent ideas, interests, and sensibilities in himself, he creates an astonishingly cohesive, unifying theory that integrates old and new, past and present. His theorizing parallels the process of eternal return of which he writes—a creative, transforming vision that expands and enriches, yet preserves the best of the old, always remaining true to the classical theorist and practitioner at the core of his work.

Since I have done an appreciative, not a critical review of Loewald, I have not dwelled on the threat to conceptual precision in such an interpretive, creative, personal approach to terminology, the possibilities for idiosyncrasy, the difficulties of comparing with other approaches. Such a unified conception may potentially mislead by what is left out and create false unity by blurring distinctions. I do not find this problem to any significant degree in Loewald, though it would take me another chapter to demonstrate this. Loewald studies what interests him; I cannot fault him for what he does not study or for what falls outside his conceptual system or metaphorical realm. Human reality *is* poetic and aesthetic, says Loewald, and theories that organize this reality cannot retreat from this ambiguity to the safer, more solid ground of the deterministic logic that is the strength of scientific method. This is not incompatible with scientific objectivity, though it may reveal the limits of it. His poetry and passion, especially in his mature work, rarely seem to me at odds with conceptual precision.

A CLOSING NOTE ON METAPSYCHOLOGY

Everything Loewald writes is obviously theoretical, not only because of its depth, density, and complexity but also because it always does what theory should do—meaningfully generalize about the way the mind and psychoanalysis work. Despite the isomorphic relationship of his model of the mind to a model of reality in the superordinate sense, Loewald has no wish to create a so-called general theory of the mind, nor does he think psychoanalysis can do so. He has, for example, the classical analyst's paradoxical preoccupation with the infantile as revealed and reconstructed in analysis while simultaneously having no interest in the "objective" data of infant observation for purposes of his theorizing. So, in a sense, Loewald's theory is *entirely* a clinical theory. This may strike one as odd, because, as I have noted, no clinical data (in the usual sense) are present. There is an absence not only of case material but also of the usual categories of experience-near clinical abstraction—generalizing about diagnostic categories, character types, or typical transferences, resistances, countertransferences, or typical etiologic constellations, interpretations, or reconstructions relevant to particular developmental epochs.

So he writes theoretical papers that rarely contain any clinical data. But to those who appreciate him, he never talks about *anything* that does not resonate directly with clinical experience. He speaks himself of the difficulty in classifying his papers according to whether they are clinical or theoretical. Consideration of this enigma has led me to conclude that Loewald may be demonstrating, perhaps unwittingly, how we may usefully recover the authentic, original meaning of the term *metapsychology*.

The reason we often give for not finding a classic psychoanalytic paper personally or clinically relevant is that it is too "theoretical." Perhaps we love Freud's "clinical" studies but find the purely "metapsychological" papers historically relevant but clinically remote, abstract. My sense is that "theoretical" and "metapsychological" are frequently simply code words that each of us uses to characterize that which we cannot relate to personal experience.

Freud often said that his theories of the mind were models and that he meant to imply no direct link whereby the mind as he conceived it could be directly derived from the positivistically conceived superordinate reality that lay "beneath" it: objective reality, the body, the brain. We tend to view this skeptically, because Freud believed that one day we would be able to make that direct link, and indeed, his paradigm, his worldview, would have naturally predicted that. But cannot Freud's psychic reality and his so-called objective reality be conceived as in the same relation to each other as I have described Loewald's theory of the mind and his worldview? May they, too, be regarded as isomorphic? This would be consistent with Loewald's paradigm, the more current, still-emerging worldview that many of us may share. In this paradigm, psychic reality and absolute reality share the same structure, cocreate and codefine each other, but neither is derived from or explains the other, or is taken to be *actually* superordinate to the other.

If we share the worldview of a sophisticated theorist, his theories will seem less obviously theories. Concepts, metaphors, symbols—all of these may function at varying degrees of distance from the realities they organize. The perfect, ideal symbol actualizes reality, seems to, *may* express reality directly. Rather than standing for something true, it may function as a vehicle for the direct realization of truth. As Winnicott points out (1953), for a devout Catholic the wafer *is* the body of Christ, a living embodiment of it, not a symbol in the sense of a simple substitute or displacement. For a devout Loewaldian, the concept of internalization may function similarly, as a tool to express something that resonates as true in our deepest selves. For many devout Freudians, the concept of psychic energy may have functioned in the same way. For Freud and his followers, notions of energy, force, structure, and mechanism were meaningful concepts that resonated as authentic at many levels. Papers that speak of libidinal flows and quantitative factors may leave a modern reader cold, but the realities referenced were not only the physicalistic entities and forces of the natural world but also the vitality and intensities of human experience.

Classic papers that seem dry and abstract may be so. Psychoanalytic journals old and new are full of unoriginal, pedantic, or derivative papers with no apparent connection to real life. But they may also *seem* so because we are relating to them as abstract categories relative to our preferred ways of understanding. We forget the probability that if the paper was truly classic—read, appreciated, and used by many analysts— it was probably directly relatable to personal analytic experience, just as Loewald's papers with their "absence of clinical data" appear to many of us. Freud was not only stretching abstract theoretical muscles in Chapter 7 to make his theory of the mind fit into an abstract energic reality. He was finding that the same metaphors that were useful in understanding the world as he knew it were helping him understand the mind of his patient and himself *as he experienced them in the deepest, most direct, actual sense in the clinical, real world.* I submit that this may be the "original meaning" of metapsychology—that which bridges or links personal experience on the one hand and the useful conceptual tools by which we may actually understand and live that experience on the other. The better the metapsychology, the more difficult to separate these factors from each other; such a theory appears to be an intuitively natural way to think about the mind, its metaphorical nature not easily visible to us.

Loewald's metapsychology functions in just such a way. We may easily forget that Loewaldian internalization is a construct, a metaphor, because it rings true on so many different levels. The concept captures the essential momentum and vitality that energy supplied to Freud's theory, and despite its comparable ambiguity, resonates more authentically to a more modern mind. That is why so many of us react so deeply and personally to his work, why we become interactive with it, find that he resonates with our own personal and theoretical pasts and presents, and why reading and rereading him constitutes not only an act of understanding but also of integration. When we understand him, we find we also understand ourselves and our work in significant new ways. This authentic function of theory in psychoanalysis is synonymous with Freud's original meaning: That which deepens our understanding raises it to a higher level.

Loewald's understanding that all metapsychology worth the name is and was metaphorically grounded in actual experience has helped him to imaginatively reconstruct, rediscover, and preserve some of the important real life that is mixed into the deadwood of our analytic past. Like good interpretations, these "ancient" truths are inescapably shaped or altered by new understandings and must be compatible with them. Loewald's boldly integrative approach helps us see things that Freud could not have imagined, let alone known; but Loewald also shows us that Freud may have known things we have forgotten, sometimes more than he himself could know he knew, and always more than we will think if we do not try to bridge the gap between Freud's conceptual language and the experiences and contexts to which they refer. Loewald not only gives us new metapsychology, he also helps us regain our roots, our metapsychological heritage.

To summarize, Loewald believes that "words, including concepts used in science, are living and enlivening entities in their authentic function" (Loewald, 1978a, p. 193). Psychoanalytic concepts can be redefined and reinterpreted, seen anew in the face of new data and ways of seeing, thus becoming transformed and transformative. Although he anticipated much of what is new in psychoanalysis in the past 30 years, he also anticipated a more recent integrative trend and a return to classical theory—a return to Freud. Staying true to apparently divergent ideas, interests, and sensibilities in himself, he created an astonishingly cohesive, unifying theory that integrates old and new, past and present. His theorizing parallels the process of eternal return of which he writes—a creative, transforming vision that expands and enriches yet remains true to the classical theorist and practitioner at the core of his work.

References

Blos, P. (1973). The epigenesis of the adult neurosis. *The Psychoanalytic Study of the Child* 27:106–135. New York: International Universities Press.

Cooper, A. M. (1986). Psychoanalysis today: new wine in old bottles. Presented at the Annual Meeting of The American Psychoanalytic Association, May.

—— (1988). Our changing views of the nature of the therapeutic action of psychoanalysis: comparing Strachey and Loewald. *Psychoanalytic Quarterly* 57:15–27.

Ferenczi, S. (1909). Introjection and transference. In *Sex in Psychoanalysis*, p. 49. New York: Brunner, 1950.

Ferenczi, S., and Rank, O. (1925). *The Development of Psychoanalysis*. New York: International Universities Press, 1986.

Ferguson, F. (1949). *The Idea of a Theater*. New York: Doubleday Anchor Books, 1953.

Fisher, Charles. (1956). Dreams, images, and perception. *Journal of American Psychoanalytic Association*, vol. 4.

Freud, S. (1894). The neuro-psychoses of defence. *Standard Edition* 3:43–61.

—— (1895a). Project for a scientific psychology. *Standard Edition* 1:283–387.

—— (1895b). *Studies of Hysteria. Standard Edition* 2.

—— (1899). Screen memories. *Standard Edition* 3:299–322.

—— (1900). *The Interpretation of Dreams. Standard Edition* 5.

—— (1915a). Instincts and their vicissitudes. *Standard Edition* 14:117–140.

—— (1915b). The unconscious. *Standard Edition* 14:159–205.

—— (1920). *Beyond the Pleasure Principle. Standard Edition* 18:3–64.

—— (1940). *An Outline of Psycho-analysis. Standard Edition* 23:139–207.

—— (1954). *The Origins of Psychoanalysis.* New York: Basic Books, p. 379f.

Freud, S., and Jung, C. G. (1974). *Briefwechsel.* Ed. William McGuire and Wolfgang Sauerländer. Frankfurt am Main: S. Fischer Verlag.

—— (1974). *The Freud/Jung Letters.* Ed. William McGuire, trans. Ralph Manheim and R. F. C. Hull. Bollingen Series 94. Princeton, NJ: Princeton University Press.

Hoffer, W. (1956). Transference and transference neurosis. *International Journal of Psycho-Analysis* 37:377.

Jones, E. (1955). *The Life and Work of Sigmund Freud,* vol. 2. London: Hogarth.

Loewald, H. W. (1951). Ego and reality. In *Papers on Psychoanalysis,* pp. 3–20. New Haven, CT: Yale University Press, 1980.

—— (1952). The problem of defense and the neurotic interpretation of reality. *Op. cit.,* pp. 21–32.

—— (1955). Hypnoid state, repression, abreaction, and recollection. *Op. cit.,* pp. 33–42.

—— (1960). On the therapeutic action of psychoanalysis. *Op. cit.,* 1980, pp. 221–256.

—— (1962). Superego and Time. *Op. cit.,* pp. 43–52.

—— (1962a). Internalization, separation, mourning, and the superego. *Psychoanalytic Quarterly* 31:483–504.

———— (1962b). The superego and ego-ideal II. Superego and time. *International Journal of Psycho-Analysis* 43:264–268.

———— (1970). Psychoanalytic theory and psychoanalytic process. In *Papers on Psychoanalysis*, pp. 277–301. New Haven, CT: Yale University Press, 1980.

———— (1971a). On motivation and instinct theory. *Op. cit.*, pp. 102–137.

———— (1971b). The transference neurosis: comments on the concept and the phenomenon. *Op. cit.*, pp. 302–314.

———— (1973). On internalization. *Op. cit.*, pp. 69–86.

———— (1975). Psychoanalysis as an art and the fantasy character of the psychoanalytic situation. *Op. cit.*, pp. 352–371.

———— (1976). Perspectives on memory. *Op. cit.*, pp. 148–173.

———— (1977). Book review essay on *The Freud/Jung Letters*. *Op. cit.*, pp. 405–418.

———— (1978a). Primary process, secondary process, and language. *Op. cit.*, pp. 178–206.

———— (1978b). *Psychoanalysis and the History of the Individual*. New Haven, CT: Yale University Press.

———— (1978c). Instinct theory, object relations, and psychic structure formation. *Op. cit.*, pp. 207–218.

———— (1979). The waning of the oedipus complex. *Op. cit.*, pp. 384–404.

———— (1980). *Papers on Psychoanalysis*. New Haven, CT: Yale University Press.

———— (1985). Oedipus complex and development of self. *Psychoanalytic Quarterly* 54:435–443.

———— (1988). *Sublimation: Inquiries into Theoretical Psychoanalysis*. New Haven, CT: Yale University Press.

Rilke, R. M. (1907). *Letters on Cézanne*. Ed. C. Rilke, trans. J. Agee. New York: Fromm International Publications. Reprinted 1985.

Ritvo, S. (1974). Current status of the concept of infantile neurosis. *The Psychoanalytic Study of the Child* 29:159–181. New York: International Universities Press.

Rycroft, C. (1956). The nature and function of the analyst's communication to the patient. *International Journal of Psycho-Analysis* 37:470.

Sandler, J. (1983). Reflections on some relations between psycho-analytic concepts and psychoanalytic practice. *International Journal of Psycho-Analysis* 64:35–45.

Silverberg, W. (1948). The concept of transference. *Psychoanalytic Quarterly* 17:321.

Spitz, R. (1956). Countertransference. *Journal of American Psycho-analytic Association*, vol. 4.

Stern, D. N. (1985). *The Interpersonal World of the Infant. A View from Psychoanalysis and Developmental Psychology.* New York: Basic Books.

Strachey, J. (1934). The nature of the therapeutic action of psycho-analysis. *International Journal of Psycho-Analysis* 15:127–159.

―――― (1937). Symposium on the theory of the therapeutic results of psycho-analysis. *International Journal of Psycho-Analysis* 18:139–145.

Tolpin, M. (1970). The infantile neurosis. *The Psychoanalytic Study of the Child* 25:273–305. New York: International Universities Press.

Tower, L. (1956). Countertransference. *Journal of the American Psychoanalytic Association*, vol. 4.

Waelder, R. (1956). Introduction to the discussion on problems of transference. *International Journal of Psycho-Analysis* 37:367.

Winnicott, D. W. (1953). Transitional objects and transitional phenomena. A study of the first not-me possession. In *Collected Papers. Through Pediatrics to Psychoanalysis*, pp. 229–243. New York: Basic Books, 1975.

Contributors

Arnold M. Cooper M.D., is Professor of Psychiatry, Cornell University Medical College and Payne Whitney Clinic, New York Hospital; Training and Supervising Analyst, Columbia University Psychoanalytic Center for Training and Research, New York. He is past president of the American Psychoanalytic Association, and is the co-editor with Otto Kernberg and Ethel Person of *Psychoanalysis: Toward the Second Century*.

Gerald I. Fogel M.D., is Associate Clinical Professor of Psychiatry, College of Physicians and Surgeons, Columbia University; Training and Supervising Analyst, Columbia University Psychoanalytic Center for Training and Research, New York. He is co-editor with Wayne Myers of *Perversion and Near-Perversion in Clinical Practice: New Psychoanalytic Perspectives*.

Lawrence Friedman M.D., is Clinical Professor of Psychiatry and a member of the History of Psychiatry section of the Department of Psychiatry, Cornell University Medical College. He is in private practice in New York and is the author of *The Anatomy of Psychotherapy.*

Hans W. Loewald M.D., is Clinical Professor of Psychiatry Emeritus, Yale University School of Medicine and was Training and Supervising Analyst, Western New England Institute for Psychoanalysis until his retirement. He is the author of *Papers on Psychoanalysis, Psychoanalysis and the History of the Individual,* and *Sublimation: Inquiries into Theoretical Psychoanalysis.*

Roy Schafer Ph.D., is Training and Supervising Analyst, Columbia University Psychoanalytic Center for Training and Research and is in private practice in New York. He is the author of *Aspects of Internalization, A New Language for Psychoanalysis, Language and Insight,* and *The Analytic Attitude.*

ACKNOWLEDGMENTS

The editor gratefully acknowledges the following for permission to reprint previously published material:

International Journal of Psychoanalysis for papers first published on the dates indicated—"On the Therapeutic Action of Psychoanalysis," vol. 41, 1960; "Superego and Time," vol. 43, 1962. All by Hans W. Loewald, M.D., copyright © by The Institute of Psycho-Analysis, London. Reprinted in *Papers on Psychoanalysis*, New Haven, CT: Yale University Press, 1980.

Journal of the American Psychoanalytic Association (published by International Universities Press, Inc.) for "Psychoanalysis as an Art and the Fantasy Character of the Psychoanalytic Situation," by Hans W. Loewald, M.D., vol. 23, 1975. Reprinted in *Papers on Psychoanalysis*, New Haven, CT: Yale University Press, 1980.

The Psychoanalytic Quarterly for papers first published on the dates indicated—"Our Changing Views of the Therapeutic Action of Psychoanalysis: Comparing Strachey and Loewald," by Arnold M. Cooper, M.D., vol. 57, 1988; "The Authentic Function of Psychoanalytic Theory: An Overview of the Contributions of Hans Loewald," by Gerald I. Fogel, M.D., vol. 58, 1989. All copyright © by The Psychoanalytic Quarterly, Inc.

Chapter 2, "On the Therapeutic Action of Psychoanalysis," by Hans W. Loewald, M.D., is based on a paper presented in two parts at meetings of the Western New England Psychoanalytic Society in 1956 and 1957. Sections I and III were read at the annual meeting of the American Psychoanalytic Association, Chicago, 1957. Section IV was read at the 20th Congress of the International Psychoanalytic Association, Paris, 1957.

Chapter 3, "Our Changing Views of the Therapeutic Action of Psychoanalysis," by Arnold M. Cooper, M.D., is a revised version of a paper presented to the Association for Psychoanalytic Medicine, New York, NY, December 2, 1986.

Chapter 6, "Superego and Time," by Hans W. Loewald, M.D., is based on a paper that developed some thoughts on the futurity of the superego and on a psychoanalytic conceptualization of time that were first adumbrated in Dr. Loewald's paper "Internalization, Separation, Mourning, and the Superego." While the two papers were published the same year (1962), "Superego and Time" was written some two years later than the original version of the other one as a contribution to the panel "The Superego and the Ego-Ideal" held at the 22nd International Psychoanalytic Congress in Edinburgh in 1961.

Chapter 7, "Psychoanalysis as an Art, and the Fantasy Character of the Psychoanalytic Situation," by Hans W. Loewald, M.D., is based on a paper delivered as the Rado Lecture at the Columbia University Psychoanalytic Clinic for Training and Research, May 21, 1974.

Chapter 8, "Transcending the Limits of Revisionism and Classicism," by Gerald I. Fogel, M.D., is based on the paper "The Authentic Function of Psychoanalytic Theory: An Overview of the Contributions of Hans Loewald." In December 1986 Dr. Fogel moderated a panel at a meeting of The Association for Psychoanalytic Medicine titled "On the Therapeutic Action of Psychoanalysis," by Hans W. Loewald: A Psychoanalytic Classic Revisited. The panelists were Arnold M. Cooper, Lawrence Friedman, and Roy Schafer. Their papers all were influential and useful to Dr. Fogel in preparing to lead a seminar on Loewald's work at the Columbia Psychoanalytic Center the following spring, out of which came the ideas that led to this chapter. Although Dr. Fogel is, of course, responsible for all that he states in this chapter, some of these ideas were expressed or touched upon by one or more of these authors on that occasion, and some of the positions Dr. Fogel takes are in relation to their positions. Dr. Fogel has noted some of the more obvious instances in this chapter.

INDEX